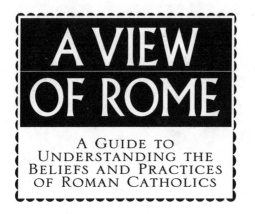

A VIEW OF ROME

A GUIDE TO UNDERSTANDING THE BELIEFS AND PRACTICES OF ROMAN CATHOLICS

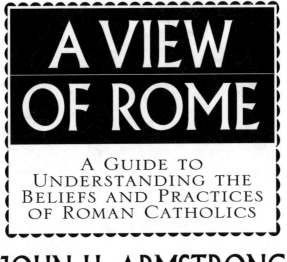

A VIEW OF ROME

A GUIDE TO UNDERSTANDING THE BELIEFS AND PRACTICES OF ROMAN CATHOLICS

JOHN H. ARMSTRONG

MOODY PRESS
CHICAGO

Moody Press, a ministry of the Moody Bible Institute,
is designed for education, evangelization, and edification.
If we may assist you in knowing more about Christ
and the Christian life, please write us without obligation:
Moody Press, c/o MLM, Chicago, Illinois 60610.

© 1995 by
JOHN ARMSTRONG

All Scripture quotations are taken from the *New American Standard Bible,* © copyright The Lockman Foundation 1960, 1962, 1963, 1968, 1971, 1972, 1973, 1975, 1977, 1994. Used by permission.

ISBN: 0-8024-9146-4

1 3 5 7 9 10 8 6 4 2

Printed in the United States of America

For the new reformation
that is desperately needed in our time

And for my first born, Matthew John Armstrong,
who has already lived his young life
in a way that honors his name,
"gift of the Lord,"
and who encourages his father and mother
as he seeks after the kingdom of God
with all his heart, mind, and soul.
He lives as a reformer who courageously pursues
God's calling upon his life.

CONTENTS

ACKNOWLEDGMENTS

The author is in continual debt to the board of Reformation & Revival Ministries, Inc., who give time, friendship, and support so that he might labor for the reformation of the church in our generation.

Special thanks to Pastor John Sale, who not only chairs the board of this ministry but serves me uniquely as a dear friend and a special brother in Christ! I thank God every day that He spared your life, for you encourage me beyond measure. May we both be stronger because we have shared in one another's lives so personally in these past few years.

Moody Press has shown continual encouragement in several projects undertaken by me and this ministry. Jim Bell gives perspective and direction; Linda Holland ministers encouragement to an easily discouraged writer; and Joe O'Day is a fine editor. Thanks again to all of you.

Very special thanks to Stacy, my lovely daughter, who serves me daily as my secretary and continually brings delight to both my life and my work.

Finally, a debt of deepest appreciation to Anita, who once again understood the deadlines, pressures, and demands of finishing another manuscript. Your input in both reading and responding to this project helped improve it in every way.

And thanks to a number of friends who gave input to this little book, helping me gain clearer focus in the writing of it. May God be pleased to bring many into a saving relationship with His Son because we shared in this work together.

INTRODUCTION

This book was birthed in response to a perceived need in the present church scene. In 1992 Moody Press asked me to edit a volume of essays by evangelical scholars regarding present Catholic and evangelical discussion. In an atmosphere of increasingly open relationship between members of our respective fellowships, we felt that a number of important issues needed to be addressed in a theologically responsible manner but with a conciliatory spirit. That volume, *Roman Catholicism: Evangelical Protestants Analyze What Divides and Unites Us* (1994), seems to have found a significant place in the current dialogue between Catholics and evangelicals. Theologians, historians, and well-trained readers have found it useful.

Because of the more academic nature of that volume, the publisher and I began to ponder some questions: What about the average member of the church? Can we write a book that will speak to the devout Christian who is confused by much that is happening in the present religious scene? More particularly, What is the evangelical who studies the Bible with a Catholic neighbor to say when the Catholic questions his or her remaining in a Protestant church? And, further, What about the Catholic who seems to have an evangelical understanding of the Christian faith and yet remains actively involved in Roman Catholicism? How do we explain important doctrinal differences in our present time in both a charitable and biblically correct manner? Does it still make a difference why we differ, or should we just sweep the Reformation and its doctrinal debates aside and get on with building a new coalition for unity?

This book will look at several areas in which Catholics and evangelicals agree. These are far more considerable in number than many realize. It will show that a new day of more conciliatory discussion presents us with an opportunity for genuinely hearing the Gospel of Christ afresh. It will also explain why the Protestant Reformation of the sixteenth century was necessary and why the beliefs that divided the church at that time still remain serious concerns for evangelical Christians today.

This book will try to focus the reader's attention on those beliefs that still genuinely divide Catholics and evangelicals. No amount of good will should be allowed to cloud concern for the truth. My greatest concern is that relativism—the idea that truth changes from person to person—may be destroying a concern for truth that once characterized both Catholics and evangelicals.

John Wesley, an ardent evangelist and Christian, published a letter to a Roman Catholic (in Dublin in 1749) in which he states my spirit quite well:

> I do not suppose all the bitterness is on your side. I know there is too much on our side also. So much that I fear many Protestants (so-called) will be angry at me, too, for writing to you in this manner, and will say, "Tis showing you too much favour; you deserve no such treatment at our hands." . . . I shall therefore endeavour, as mildly and inoffensively as I can, to remove in some measure the ground of your unkindness by plainly declaring what our belief and what our practice is.

In this spirit and with this purpose I invite you into this book.

PART ONE

THE HISTORICAL HERITAGE

The Christian church was not always divided by many of the barriers and disagreements that now exist. Though persecutions threatened to destroy the young church, she grew stronger with every wave of attack. Heresies and schisms threatened her almost from the beginning, but the visible church remained virtually one until a great division between East and West in the eleventh century.

In the sixteenth century another great division came to the Western church when Rome, then the political and religious center of the magisterial church, excommunicated an Augustinian monk named Martin Luther and set off the Protestant Reformation. Finally, at the Council of Trent (1545–1563), Rome closed the door on the theological contributions of the Reformers, who sought to correct serious errors that had evolved over the previous two centuries.

What brought about this great divide, and why do evangelicals not simply "go back to Rome" now that Vatican II has offered an olive branch by naming them as "separated brethren?"

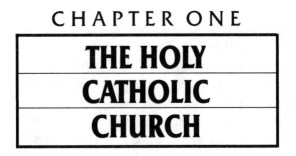

CHAPTER ONE

THE HOLY
CATHOLIC
CHURCH

I believe in God the Father Almighty, Maker of heaven and earth; and in Jesus Christ His only Son, our Lord, who was conceived by the Holy Spirit, born of the virgin Mary, suffered under Pontius Pilate, was crucified, dead, and buried; He descended into hell; the third day He rose from the dead; He ascended into heaven, and sitteth on the right hand of God the Father Almighty; from thence He shall come to judge the living and the dead.

I believe in the Holy Spirit; the holy catholic Church, the communion of saints; the forgiveness of sins; the resurrection of the body; and the life everlasting. Amen.

These are the familiar words of the Apostles' Creed, a historic and simple summary of basic truths confessed by early Christians. Though most certainly not the direct product of the twelve apostles of Christ, it is commonly agreed that this short creed is a *summary* statement of the apostles' teaching. It is in harmony with the spirit of the New Testament.

Most Catholics know this creed well. They are often surprised to hear Protestants quote it. Likewise, some evangelicals are equally surprised when they hear fellow evangelicals recite it. Often evangelicals are even more surprised to discover that here is an ancient creed that is not so much an abstract and mysterious document as a living, vibrant, profession of essential truths believed by all Christians over the centuries.

Here we have a universal starting point for Christian affirmation. A creed expressing vital, foundational Christian truths confessed by believers long before the rupture of the visible church in the sixteenth century. But all that needs to be confessed is not in this creed. Nothing, for example, regarding grace or the authority of Scripture is found here. Nevertheless, it is a beginning—a starting point for all *historic* Christian confession.

Living trust in Christ requires that Christian faith be rooted in history as well as in present experience. True confession cannot exist without the New Testament itself, and the New Testament requires that we confess allegiance to Christ, both to His person and His work. All who profess love for Christ need to understand this.

"But wait a minute," you say. "I am an evangelical Christian. I cannot confess that I believe in the 'holy catholic Church.' That language is not acceptable to me. I believe in a biblical, New Testament church, but not a *holy catholic* church."

Through the centuries believers have confessed their faith by asserting that they believe in the holy catholic church. This is not anti-evangelical language. It was our Lord who constituted His church as a holy catholic church when He said, "I will build My church; and the gates of Hades will not overpower it" (Matthew 16:18). This often disputed text asserts that Jesus is committed to His church. Because the church is His, it is *holy,* or "set apart" from ordinary purposes. Because it is a church spread over the whole earth, encompassing peoples of every background, both ethnically and socially (see Revelation 5:9), it is a *catholic* (meaning "universal") church.

When we use the words *Roman Catholic,* however, we are talking about something else, namely, a communion linked to the historic authority and practice of Rome. That is why the abbreviated name *Catholic* is properly capitalized when it is used in this book with reference to the *Roman* Catholic Church. In this case *Catholic* is being used of a particular communion of people, not as a reference to all Christians who make up the universal, or catholic, church of Christ.

ONE FAITH ... ONE LORD ... ONE CHURCH?

The apostle Paul confessed the affirmation "one body [church] ... one Lord, one faith" (Ephesians 4:4–5). Though Christians have differing beliefs of what the visible church should look like, they agree that there is a universal church in the world.

The word *Catholic* (when referring to Roman Catholicism) is a relatively recent term. Until the sixteenth century it was simply "the church." Sometimes it would be "the church catholic." Not until some years after the Protestant Reformation did the church, historically based in Rome, begin to use the title "Catholic" to distinguish itself from the Protestant movement. The church, headquartered in Vatican City, with its argument for the succession of apostles back to Peter, became the Roman Catholic Church. This name distinguished itself not only from European Protestantism but from another branch of Christendom—the Eastern Orthodox Church, with its many similarities to the Roman Catholic Church, excepting loyalty to the papacy and the requirement of celibacy for its priests.

Further, when the Evangelical Alliance was formed in the United States in 1867, it adopted a nine-point doctrinal statement based on its English counterpart, which expressed a similar understanding of our essential agreement in early church history. It included the following:

> Resolved, that in the same spirit we propose no new creed, but taking broad, historical, and Evangelical catholic ground, we solemnly reaffirm and profess our faith in all the doctrines of the inspired word of God, and in the consensus of doctrines as held by all true Christians from the beginning. And we do more especially affirm our belief in the divine-human person and atoning work of our Lord and Savior Jesus Christ as the only and sufficient source of salvation, as the heart and soul of Christianity, and as the center of all true Christian union and fellowship. (Schaff and Herzog, 4:222)

The World Evangelical Fellowship, formed in our present century, represents various associations of regional and national fellowships of evangelical churches. It stands in the same tradition of thought by confessing, in part, the following: "We believe in . . . the unity of the Spirit of all true believers, the church, the body of Christ."

What is meant by these evangelical Christian affirmations when they speak of the church as *catholic*? And what is meant by the modifiers "broad, historical, and Evangelical catholic ground" used in the above statement? To answer that question we need to consider the doctrinal unity that came to the historic church in the first five centuries following the death of Christ and the apostles.

THE HISTORIC CONSENSUS: ITS IMPORTANCE

The visible church of Jesus Christ sought from its very beginning to maintain its essential oneness in teaching and life. In the midst of a hostile and anti-Christian culture, this was vital to its strength. Opposition from outside the church threatened it with intense periods of persecution, as various Roman emperors came and went over the centuries. Ten bloody seasons of persecution resulted.

The overall effect of these attempts to stop the growth of the church was a continual purifying of the church from nominal professions of faith. This ultimately brought deep and lasting growth in both power and influence. As the old saying goes, "The blood of the martyrs was the seed of the church!"

What threatened the church even more in these early centuries was error from within. The infant movement was threatened with compromise and heresy. The visible body of Christ on earth was distressed repeatedly by serious heresies. What did the leadership of the young church do to counteract this insidious virus within her?

Over the first four centuries a number of councils were convened to address these doctrinal errors. Bishops (presbyters, or leaders of churches and groups of churches) met at important cities for months at a time to consider important doctrinal and moral issues facing the church. Some of these councils were called for political reasons. Others became, quite honestly, platforms for leaders whose motives were not always noble. Yet through it all, God's providence overruled. God the Holy Spirit was at work guiding the church into a fuller and deeper understanding of the essential truths that would protect the message of Christ and His apostles from errors that would destroy it.

It is not surprising that in the early centuries the church addressed these kinds of problems so directly. Had not the apostle

Paul written, "According to the grace of God which was given to me, like a wise master builder I laid a foundation, and another is building on it. . . . For no man can lay a foundation other than the one which is laid, which is Jesus Christ" (1 Corinthians 3:10–11)? The foundation of the church was Christ. About this there must be no lingering doubt. What made Christianity a vital religion in the ancient Roman culture was the uniqueness of its founder—both His unique person and His unique work. To build on any foundation other than Christ Jesus was, simply put, to invite disaster. It was to build with wood, hay, and straw, not gold, silver, and precious stones (see verse 12).

The early history of the church followed Paul's pattern. It built a solid confessional foundation. This foundation was laid by these early councils and creeds. Affirmation followed affirmation, and denial followed denial. These all were necessary if the church was to be faithful to the work of the apostles—namely, the New Testament Scriptures themselves.

These historic councils addressed matters such as the discipline of ministers, schism, and doctrinal heresies. The principal heresies addressed in these early centuries dealt with matters related to the person of Jesus Christ. Was He really God? Was He truly man? How are we to understand the triune nature of the Godhead in light of Christ being eternal God, yet distinct from the Father, who is also eternal God? And what is the relationship of the Holy Spirit to the Father and the Son?

ROMAN CATHOLICS AND EVANGELICALS

Catholics and evangelicals share a consistent loyalty to the creeds of these early orthodox fathers and theologians. When the Protestant Reformation took place in the sixteenth century, there was never a serious battle over any of these great truths that had united the church for centuries. There is still much we share together in these bedrock foundational beliefs.

Since the turn of this century much of Protestantism has turned more and more away from these historic Christian statements of faith. In more recent years that same liberal virus has infected

Catholic theologians and, with them, many parish priests as well. We live in an era quite different from the way things used to be. In the past we could have assumed that all Catholics and Protestants agreed on the orthodox creedal statements from the first five or six centuries. But that has changed. Modernist ministers and priests have jettisoned truths once held by all who named Christ in our traditions. And that has confused many church members.

Our young people go away to Catholic and Protestant schools only to have essential Christian truths undermined by professors who are financially supported by the families and churches of these children. What is happening? A twentieth-century error has influenced both Catholics and evangelicals. It attacks almost everything previously assumed as part and parcel of the historic Christian faith. This has caused many Catholics and evangelicals to realize that we have a new common enemy. Both secularism and materialism threaten to bring down Western culture. Moral chaos abounds, both in personal lives and in society at large.

In the face of this challenge, especially in Europe and the United States, Catholics and evangelicals are increasingly talking about the common enemies of their faith. We are finding out that we agree on most of the writings of the early church fathers and the councils and creeds of Christendom. This often comes as a surprise to people on both sides of the Reformation. The result has been a growing awareness of our need to work together in areas where we are being attacked by forces that are distinctly related to twentieth-century life.

Protestant evangelicals need to understand that we confess a continuity of truth through the ages and that these early church creeds are gifts to us. Certainly we subject them to the authority of Scripture, as we will see in chapter 5, but we believe that much of what Scripture teaches, especially regarding the nature of God and Christ, is *plainly defended and set forth* by these ancient creeds.

Evangelicals share more than a few vital biblical truths with Catholics. We seek to cultivate a *distinctly* Christian worldview. We both believe—if we reject the modernist criticism now present in our respective traditions—that the Bible is the inerrant Word of God. We are consistent supernaturalists who believe in the doctrines of the Trinity, the deity and humanity of Christ, and the bodily resurrection of Christ. We confess faith in His ascension into heaven and in His future bodily return. We believe in life after the grave and in the judgment that follows. We even sing some of the same songs, use the same biblical texts in our public worship, practice intercessory prayer, and develop a spiritual life grounded on faith in Christ.

Catholics need to understand that evangelicals are not radicals who broke away from the ancient faith of the church. Luther, Calvin, and the early Protestant Reformers strongly affirmed their loyalty to the creeds and went far to demonstrate that they were true heirs of the early church. This is precisely why we still have so much in common. Evangelical faith is not novel. It is not anti-catholic faith, given how the historic church has understood catholicism. The Reformers never dreamed of "throwing out" historic affirmations in whole or in part.

What the early Protestant Reformers did do was to challenge a church authority that they believed contradicted itself. There is a world of difference in both spirit and practice between reactionaries and reformers. They believed, quite simply, that the visible church had gone beyond the authority of Scripture. They further asserted that the gospel had been lost through the evolution of doctrine. This evolution so corrupted the visible church, according to the Reformers, that complete reformation in vital areas of faith and practice was the only solution.

In this book we will consider what caused this Reformation and what doctrinal areas were at the heart of the divide. We will ask, "Does it still matter?" and, further, "How should evangelicals and Catholics address these differences in a new atmosphere that invites better understanding and greater tolerance?"

CHAPTER TWO

THE
DARK
AGES?

A s the church moved beyond the early centuries into the era of the medieval world, several things began to change, both in the world and in the church. In this chapter we will consider these shifts and how they prepared the way for the great divide that would come in the sixteenth century.

Evangelicals often think of the medieval era as a time of spiritual darkness across much of Europe. It is thought that the church was cold, lifeless, and dead. That the true story is quite different surprises such people.

In the early centuries the church was a persecuted minority. By the time it entered the medieval world it was an aggressive component of the establishment. This shift had begun with the conversion of Emperor Constantine in the early fourth century. By the eighth and ninth centuries, the church had won its battle with pagan culture, and its thought and life became associated with the cause of victory. Triumph brought with it a distinct theological emphasis upon the language of victory over the devil, sin, and death! It also brought the related problems of ecclesiastical triumphalism, a kind of celebrative spirit connected with victory over others.

Regarding these developments, historian D. Clair Davis concludes, "Though conditioned by the church's history, this theology of the early church faithfully reflected an important aspect of the biblical teaching of salvation. It stressed redemption—how God delivers His people from their bondage into the freedom of life with Him" (Armstrong, 45).

As the old Roman Empire broke up and more familial ways of thinking and living developed in Europe, people became concerned about right thinking regarding their personal relationship to God and to the church. As surely as the doctrines of God, Christ, man, and sin had occupied the attention of the early centuries, so now the church would address in a more focused way the doctrine of salvation. How was the great disruption between man and God to be resolved? How do I enter into fellowship with an offended, holy God?

All this led to considerable discussion of the doctrine of the atonement—the nature and design of Christ's death and how God redeems lost human beings—by the church's best theologians. The development of the church's thinking followed a discernible path—from God and Christ, to humanity and sin, and finally to grace and salvation.

Humanity's fall, the resulting depraved nature, and the need of divine grace had all been considerably debated in Augustine's response to Pelagius. Augustine, a bishop in North Africa, was an important theologian. Pelagius, also a significant figure in this era, was a fifth-century heretic who denied the necessity of sovereign grace in salvation precisely because he failed to properly understand the biblical teaching of the bondage of the human will to sin. Augustine became the champion of reigning grace precisely because he so clearly understood the nature of sin and its effects upon human beings.

Two Theologians of Importance

Anselm, the Archbishop of Canterbury (ca. 1033–1109), is perhaps best known for his insistence that Christian reason must trace its journey back to faith in Christ in order to determine what it knows and understands. Philosophic speculation could not help the church unless it was submitted properly to faith. By this he meant, simply, "I do not seek to understand that I may believe, but I believe that I may understand: for this I also believe, that unless I believe I will not understand."

Anselm contributed significantly to the historically developing doctrine of the Atonement. He argues in his classic book *Cur Deus Homo* (*Why the God-Man?*) from the facts of the Incarnation and the Cross back to God's purpose in sending Christ and the reason for His death. The uniqueness of the person who died at Calvary requires that the event—that is, His sacrificial death—be unique as well. Only Christ as the God-man could bear the wrath of God and pay the full penalty of sin. Because God is holy, sin violates His honor. Because His honor is violated, His wrath is just and perfect. Because of His wrath, sinners must have a perfect atonement made for them.

As in many theological conflicts through the ages, orthodox views often engender rival views. In the case of Anselm, his chief antagonist was Peter Abelard (1079–1142). Abelard was a scholastic philosopher and theologian who sought to reconcile faith and reason. For Abelard "the value of the Atonement was in the individual's personal response to what Christ had done for him. As he came to appreciate and bow in gratitude at the extent of God's love for him, he would respond in turn with his own love to the God who had loved him so much" (Armstrong, 48).

Does God require satisfaction, or payment, in order for sin to be atoned for? Or is the Cross merely a display of the love of God, a point of persuasive appeal for people to trust Christ? Put another way, is the Cross a place where God *actually* redeems lost men and women by atoning for their sin?

Evangelical Christians have always insisted that the love of God is demonstrated by the Cross. Many of our hymns reveal this truth. But we also insist, with Anselm and his theological tradition, that the love of Calvary is not simply a generic display of deep affection for humanity. It is a specific and particular action taken by God to actually remove His holy wrath from those He saves through the death of His Son. This is done by the Father, mysteriously, pouring out all His wrath upon His Son.

One hymn writer, Philip P. Bliss, captures this understanding well:

> "Man of Sorrows," what a name
> For the Son of God, who came
> Ruined sinners to reclaim!
> Hallelujah! what a Savior!
>
> Bearing shame and scoffing rude,
> In my place condemned He stood;
> Sealed my pardon with His blood;
> Hallelujah! what a Savior!
>
> Guilty, vile, and helpless we;
> Spotless Lamb of God was He;
> "Full atonement" can it be?
> Hallelujah! what a Savior!
>
> Lifted up was He to die,
> "It is finished," was His cry;
> Now in heav'n exalted high;
> Hallelujah! what a Savior!
>
> (1875)

"WHAT MUST I DO TO BE SAVED?"

Human beings must be brought face-to-face with God's wrath and their own sin. When, by the Spirit, this happens, they cry in deep anguish, "What must I do to be saved?" (Acts 16:30). During the Middle Ages the church sought to apply an objective theology of the Atonement to the subjective question, "How can I lay hold of what Christ has done in His death? How can I make this event my own?"

Over the preceding centuries the church had answered this question by increasingly encouraging penitent believers to look to the sacraments of the church. The reasoning went like this: Christ had died. He had given His authority to the bishops of the church, especially the bishop of Rome, who some later argued was Peter's successor. Here the power to bind and loose people from their sins was inherent. This power was given to the bishops who in turn gave it to the priests who presided over the sacraments.

The sacrament of baptism, where grace was first received, was critical to bringing one into a relationship with Christ and His church. The Supper (or Mass, as it was eventually called) was the central channel of grace for all baptized believers who wished to receive grace and remain savingly united with Christ. But receiving the Mass would not, in itself, save a person. There must be true faith and repentance in the heart. Grace must be received in a proper (worthy) manner. But that implies that salvation comes by human effort, not by grace. As a result of this type of thought, medieval theologians developed what was conceived to be an indispensable sacrament for coming properly to the Mass—penance.

In penance the faithful had their repentance made whole and complete. Inadequate repentance was changed—through penance it became heartfelt, real, complete. The same was true for faith. Small or weak faith—we might even say superficial faith—becomes genuine love through penance. This transformation might not even be perceptible, but it was real.

This whole concept, which had developed in the Monastic movement, wherein men consecrated themselves to a life of sacrifice and suffering, was intended to help people fulfill Paul's injunction to "put off" and "put on" the old life (see Colossians 3:8–17).

Penance was intended to change behavior, but in time it was identified with punishment for what the confessing person had already done. In many ways it became a virtual synonym for repentance, but with a legalistic bent. People began to travel to holy sites to observe ancient relics and in general to strive for greater holiness in order to receive grace. Eventually substitute penances were devised that relied on a monetary payment to the church. These were called indulgences. They were often used for the removal of future sins.

D. Clair Davis is helpful once again. He summarizes the problem well:

25

Technically, only the temporal penalty for sin was being dealt with (the punishment due sin this side of eternity, including that endured in purgatory), but for practical purposes that was all that anyone knew about anyway. Knowledge that one's eternal punishment had been dealt with (the assurance of salvation) was available in any case only to those few—the saints—to whom it had been revealed by extraordinary revelation. The gap that penance was devised to bridge was, in the end, still a great chasm: How can a weak sinner come to a holy Christ? (Armstrong, 50)

First, the medieval church said a person was saved by receiving grace in the Mass *if* the person had sincere faith and repentance. But when the penitent asked the question "Is my faith and repentance sincere?" he could not know for sure. To solve this problem, he or she added penance. But what if his penance was incomplete, his faith not genuinely holy? The answer was this: if his or her faith was at least sincere, he would be granted what was called "congruous grace," the grace God gives to those who are sincerely trying to please Him. "But how can I know that I am sincere?" With this approach, there can be no real assurance of salvation. The great theologian Augustine had written of election and predestination, of an invisible church made up of those who truly know the grace of God. "But how can I know that I am truly a part of the body of Christ?"

What resulted from all this was the desire to do one's best with the most sincere effort possible. Unintentionally salvation had become the joint effort of grace and human effort. And theology, the study of God and His revelation, appeared as "unknowable . . . an irrelevant puzzle" (Armstrong, 56).

THE PROBLEM OF INDULGENCES

All this led to the spark that finally lit the fire of the Reformation—the sale and commercialization of indulgences. To understand this we need a better comprehension of the medieval mind-set behind it. If nothing else, the church was consistent with medieval theology in its development of the doctrine and practice of indulgences.

What, exactly, was behind the sale of indulgences to ordinary Catholics? The medieval church's definition of sin (which to a large extent still exists in today's Catholic Church) helps to answer this question. If a person died with mortal sin (murder, adultery, even missing Mass, and so on), he or she was on the road to perdition. Mortal sin kills the life of grace begun in baptism, though confession may bring back the life of grace. Unconfessed venial sins (lying, petty theft, unkind words, and so on) meant that the person would need to spend time in purgatory, a place for cleansing (purging) from remaining sin.

All sins, even those confessed and absolved by the priest, incur a debt of temporal punishment, a finite amount of time to be spent in purgatory. It is here that indulgences came powerfully into the picture. Jesus Christ, the Blessed Mother, and the saints are all believed to have earned an abundance of merit through their holy lives. From this excess of stored merit believers might receive additional help. This help could be received through certain prayers, the veneration of relics, and the use of religious articles, such as rosaries, crucifixes, and medals.

During the Middle Ages paying money to the church for indulgences would also bring divine help. This money would not only assist the cause of the faithful giver but would assist the church in her work of mission. It was the admitted abuse of this practice that led to the steps taken by Martin Luther that precipitated the great divide in the Western church.

SUMMING UP

The decline of medieval Christianity was gradual. The more serious errors came in the fourteenth and fifteenth centuries. The results of this descending darkness were serious. Even before the career of Martin Luther in the early 1500s, Gregory of Rimini (a monk) and Thomas Bradwardine, the Archbishop of Canterbury, challenged the whole notion of synthesis in regard to salvation. What arose was a return by some to Augustine's insistence upon the sovereign grace of God conquering people's sinful rebellion. These theologians reasoned that, if one relied upon sincere cooperative efforts with God and the church, in the end it was not grace that saved. Reliance upon various kinds of preparation for grace was viewed as a form of self-righteous human effort. God did not need help, even sincere human help, to save the sinner.

Out of this theological confusion and corrupt practice the medieval church began to face serious abuses. So a providential historical context of criticism, which helped bring about the great change, was already in place when Luther began to speak out regarding the matter of indulgences.

But the changes that were needed eventually issued in a sad division. Catholics do not think that this division was necessary. Evangelicals, however, believe that the reforming of the historic Christian church led to this division because Catholicism refused to make the necessary changes in both doctrine and practice.

CHAPTER THREE

THE GREAT EVANGELICAL RECOVERY

The sixteenth-century Reformation was much more than a movement for the purification of practices. It precipitated changes that forever altered the church. To think of the Protestant Reformation as anything other than a revival of historic Christianity is to miss a vital truth. Modern evangelicals are the heirs of this Reformation.

Roman Catholics are inclined to think of the Reformation as a great disruption. They believe that, at best, the Reformers rejected the church Christ established, if not Christ Himself. And over what? Practices that were later corrected by the Catholic Counter-Reformation itself.

This perception of the events of the sixteenth century is shallow and inadequate, both historically and theologically. Though the Reformation may have been initially ignited by Luther's challenges regarding indulgences, it very quickly became a sweeping challenge to the entire religious synthesis of the Middle Ages.

THE BASIS OF THE CHALLENGE

The Reformers broke with Rome because they rejected the Christianity of the Middle Ages, a synthetic faith that failed to bring peace to their souls and the assurance of God's grace as the sole ground of their salvation. As they studied the text of the Greek New Testament, thanks to the scholarly work of Desiderius Erasmus, a Renaissance Humanist, they found Rome's message of salvation unsatisfactory. In light of the clear message of

Scripture, they came to peace with God. Modern readers must not fail to appreciate how profound this challenge really was.

Throughout the Middle Ages many reformations had occurred within the life of the church. But none drove such a deep chasm as this. These earlier movements were primarily interested in moral reform. Abuses of institutional and personal life were addressed. The Protestant Reformation began as another reforming movement for the moral life of the church. But the essence of its thrust became, within two to three years, radically doctrinal. Even by 1520, less than three years after Luther had challenged the abusive sale of indulgences, he focused his concerns on important doctrinal issues in two of his most important tracts: *The Babylonian Captivity of the Church*, and *The Appeal to the German Nobility*.

Philip Melanchthon, a friend of Luther's, summarized the Protestant concerns in the Augsburg Confession (1530), stating very positively the Protestant position regarding the important theological issues at stake. John Calvin, a second-generation Protestant Reformer, argued most clearly for a complete reformation of the church in his classic work *The Institutes of the Christian Religion*. This became the most significant systematic theology of the entire evangelical cause.

Why did the evangelicals of the sixteenth century feel compelled to move outside the Roman Church? It was not a rash decision on their part. According to the accepted theology of their time, they were cutting themselves off from the grace of God, an act that could potentially destroy them spiritually. This was their birth church. It was the church that had nursed their immortal souls. It was the visible communion of faith. What would make them leave—and at such great sacrifice? Historian Robert Godfrey answers this question:

> Historians . . . have given attention to the political, social, and economic circumstances of the sixteenth century to understand the setting of the Reformation. They have studied the cultural and intellectual developments of the late medieval and Renaissance periods as crucial backdrop for the Reformation. But ultimately it was not

these factors that divided the church. These factors may have contributed in a variety of ways to the success of the Reformation, but they were not the heart of the Reformation. The heart of the Reformation was a *distinct spiritual and theological vision*—quite different from the one that had dominated the medieval church. (Armstrong, 65; italics added)

THE LINE IN THE SAND

The defining issues of the evangelical movement are not that difficult to determine. Nor are they so numerous to be simply observed. As theologians both wrote and preached, important issues surfaced. It was not long before the genuinely significant matters were plainly stated and the lines drawn that determined the direction of both parties.

Today many respond, "Of course Luther was right. The church had made some big mistakes, and it still does. But that doesn't make the whole Roman Catholic system wrong, does it?" In a system as all-encompassing as that of the Roman Church, an attack upon any of its well-entrenched practices involved an attack upon the whole. This was the medieval way of thinking. Only in a postmodern pluralistic age like our own, where hardly any single truth is consistently confessed nor carefully connected to other truths, would we think otherwise.

When Luther asked "What is an indulgence and of what value is it?" this led logically to a full discussion of the sacrament of Penance. This challenge, as we saw in the last chapter, called into question the Roman Catholic doctrine of salvation. His question "Can the pope grant an indulgence and what kind of indulgence can he grant?" led immediately to the more profound question "What is the nature of papal authority?" And these questions led back to the ultimate challenge: "What is the church?"

The course the Reformation took in its early days followed this line of reasoning consistently. Luther was urged to silence while the church prepared a reply to his challenges. In 1518 he met at Augsburg with a papal delegation, and here Cardinal Cajetan demanded that he recant. Luther said that he could not do that unless his writings were shown to be false by the plain teaching of

Scripture. A short truce followed, but in 1519 Luther was publicly attacked by Eck, a papal theologian. Luther was asked to support Eck's traditional view that divine power was inherit in the papacy. Luther refused, saying that the pope's power was of human right, not divine. To support this he developed an important thesis that he drew from earlier theologians such as Augustine: *The Church is in reality a spiritual fellowship of all those who truly believe in Christ.* It was here that Luther demonstrated that popes and councils had erred. It struck a blow that rocked the medieval system at its foundation.

After Luther was denounced by Eck, he was threatened with excommunication by the church. His writings were condemned as "heretical, erroneous, or offensive to pious ears." His writings were to be found, wherever possible, and publicly burned. In response, on December 10, 1520, Luther publicly burned in a bonfire a copy of the document of excommunication (called a "bull") in front of the entire student body of the University of Wittenberg. His actual excommunication followed on January 2, 1521. Even before this, Luther had already voluntarily left the church, declaring that the pope was "antichrist" and that Rome had become a "nest of the devil."

THE TURNING POINT

Luther had reached the place where there was no turning back. The line had been drawn. But why? What was the turning point for this previously devout and loyal monk?

The Leipzig debate with Eck in the summer of 1519 had emboldened Luther considerably. He had come to see that his growing disagreement with the papal church was not simply a matter of indulgences and moral abuses. In tract after tract, written in Latin for scholars and in German for the people, he attacked the teachings of the medieval church that he believed undermined the two principle concerns that drove him on—the authority of the believer and the church, and the nature of grace and faith as it relates to salvation.

Luther's understanding of certain doctrines was developing as he studied the Bible more carefully. Some of his views probably never matured as they might have if he had listened to other Reformers more carefully. He was a singularly courageous and bold man, often given to strong statements and radical actions. His language is notoriously rough and coarse at times, but this belonged to the spirit of his age. He was just the man needed at this time. His style, wrote one historian, was "bold, rugged, picturesque and wonderfully clear." His words were those spoken by the average German. His writings, therefore, were in eager demand. Even in France and England, where his works were published in Latin, people read Luther.

But what teachings brought about the irreconcilable division that remains with us nearly five hundred years later? Perhaps, after all this time, we have changed sufficiently in our understanding of these vital doctrines that we can now openly heal the breach brought about by this so-called "wild boar" of the German vineyard. Perhaps we can forge a "common mission" in this age of secular humanism if our differences are no longer as large as in Luther's time. This seems to be the view of many in our day.

TWO VITAL TRUTHS

As previously noted, Luther and the Protestant evangelicals believed that two important truths stood at the heart of their reforming effort. Modern readers need to understand why these two truths are vital to the life of the church itself.

These two issues are still central to the theological differences between evangelicals and Roman Catholics. They are what we call the *formal* and *material* principles of the Reformation. It is imperative that we understand these two vital truths, for, if Rome is correct on these points, then the Protestant Reformers were wrong. But if the Protestant Reformers got it right, then the Reformation is certainly not over, and talk of formal agreement at the core of our beliefs cannot proceed.

The Formal Principle of the Reformation

We call it the formal principle because it is the thing that forms and shapes. It determines what Christians believe and why. The popular catch phrase for this principle is "Scripture alone." What that means is that the church cannot preach, teach, command, or practice anything contrary to Scripture, even for very good and necessary reasons. The church's authority is not inherently in itself but is rather derived from the written Scriptures alone. The church's task is simple—pass along to the faithful what the Scriptures teach and nothing else!

It is necessary that we understand what the evangelicals did *not* mean by this principle. First, individuals are not free to decide for themselves what to believe. They are obligated to the Scriptures. They cannot, willy-nilly, pick and choose their authority. Further, this principle did not mean that each individual Christian could interpret the Bible as he or she pleased, in opposition to the consensus of the church and its concerns over the centuries. Luther, in typically blunt fashion, wrote, "Each man could go to hell in his own way." By this he meant, go ahead and fashion your own *private* doctrines from the text. Realize, however, that such may well damn you if you conclude falsely regarding the doctrines of Christ and salvation, the central and clear concern of all holy Scripture.

The Reformers were quite concerned to demonstrate that what they taught was not something they just discovered in the sixteenth century. They sought to show how their teachings were in harmony with the Fathers of the early church, especially the great theologian Augustine. They believed that they were rediscovering something old—lost by a corrupt Rome. Though *complete* agreement with the church's consensus was not required for every doctrine, all teaching must be submitted in humility to the communion of saints with a clear demonstration that this was in fact the teaching of the Bible.

Although it is true that different Protestant communions came to differing conclusions on some important matters, such as the nature of communion and baptism, it is *not* true that they differed in the *fundamental* principles of the Reformation. When they challenged the claim that tradition was a source of revelation alongside the written Scriptures, they were in unanimous agreement. When

Rome claimed that teaching authority lay in the magisterium (the teaching office of the Catholic Church), with the pope as its chief shepherd under Christ, they were unanimous in their opposition. Against the Catholic claim of continued revelation through the church they pressed the truth of the sufficiency of Scripture.

But, said the Catholic apologists, even with an inerrant and sufficient Bible, you still don't have an infallible teacher. The Protestant Reformers answered this objection by using the arguments of Catholic humanists such as Erasmus to show how popes and councils in the Middle Ages had made contradictory claims. As Michael Horton has said,

> The best way to guard a true interpretation of Scripture, the Reformers insisted, was neither to naively embrace the infallibility of tradition, nor the infallibility of the individual, but to recognize the *communal* interpretation of Scripture. The best way to ensure faithfulness to the text is to read it together, not only with the churches of our own time and place, but with the wider "communion of saints" down through the ages. (Armstrong, 253)

The community of a church might even err, but there will always be much wisdom in many counselors (see Proverbs 11:14). We are most likely to get the meaning of Scripture right when we come to it believing that the text is infallible and we are not!

But what is the message of the Bible? Granting its infallibility and final authority for faith and practice we must ask, What does the Bible teach? Put very plainly, How am I saved and reconciled to God? Surely this is *the* question that we must all have answered if we are to know and serve Christ powerfully.

The Material Principle of the Reformation

The longing of every devout person who lived before Christ came was expressed in the question "How can I know God?" Israel's hope and consolation was in the promise of a coming deliverer, a Messiah. Her temple services, sacrificial system, and carefully developed priesthood, her unusual prophets and royal kings, all of these pointed to something, or Someone, superior to all the shadows and types of the ritualistic system. All Christians agree that this person was Jesus Christ. Here is the "desire of every nation," as the hymn writer puts it.

But how am I made right with God in Jesus Christ? How do I know that I have come into the salvation that He brings? Very simply, "What must I do to be saved?" (Acts 16:30). The answer is given by the apostle Paul: "Believe in the Lord Jesus, and you will be saved, you and your household" (v. 31). Paul says the same thing in unmistakably clear language in Romans: "But to the one who does not work, but believes in Him who justifies the ungodly, his faith is credited as righteousness" (4:5).

The Reformers referred to this doctrine of justification as "the article by which the church stands or falls." By this they did not mean that a person was saved by virtue of understanding the full ramifications of this great truth. He or she was saved by faith in Christ alone, and that through grace alone. But here the visible church must stand on Christ alone as the sole basis for justification before a holy God, or it will fall. A person who *truly* trusts Christ alone will be saved, whether he or she understands this article *fully* or not. (Who can fully understand any article of truth?)

The Reformers never tired of insisting that justification was a legal (forensic) concept. The term *justification* was the term of a law court. It was the word that described a change in status. It was the opposite of "guilty" or "condemned." To be justified was, very simply, to be right with God. Nothing could be added to this status and nothing subtracted.

The Reformers often spoke of justification as resting entirely upon the merits of Jesus Christ alone. We rest, they argued, upon the obedience of Christ, which is imputed to us on the basis of our faith in Him alone. We do not grow into this grace or find favor with God over time as we experience the impartation of new life to our souls. We are immediately accepted by God, fully and finally, on the basis of Christ and His work for us.

Rome's argument was, and still is, that Christ's righteousness is infused into the believer's heart, wherein a process begins that leads to final justification. Jerome, the producer of the Latin Vulgate translation of the Bible, actually translated the Greek word that meant "to *declare* righteous" as "to *make* righteous." When Greek scholars challenged this in the pre-Reformation era, it, in effect, pried open the door for a better understanding of Scripture itself. When Luther came to see this truth, he said, "It was as if the windows of heaven were flung open and I was born again." So he was.

SUMMING UP

The Reformers believed that the Church of Rome had abandoned these two vital principles. The first principle they saw in Scripture and the Fathers. The second, though not as plainly developed in the early church, they saw in budlike form in Augustine's teaching, especially with regard to the sovereignty of grace in salvation and the priority of God's will in granting faith to those who believe. They insisted that on both counts the Scriptures agreed with them and that doctrinal reform based on the plain teaching of the Word of God was needed. This meant that the teaching and practices developed in the late Middles Ages by scholastic theologians had to go.

How did Rome respond to this serious challenge? To that we now turn.

CHAPTER FOUR

A
FALLEN
CHURCH

I f the Reformers were correct, Rome was a falling church in the era prior to the Protestant Reformation. She had departed from the authority and sufficiency of Scripture. Centuries of extrabiblical tradition, as well as practices that were nonapostolic, had led her progressively away from the simplicity of New Testament Christianity. She had also departed from the gospel of grace, though her theologians tried to demonstrate otherwise. How did the church *officially* reply to these charges that she had departed from both Scripture and the gospel?

These were extremely serious charges. We are not considering minor issues that churches sometimes dispute. The apostle Paul wrote to the Galatian church that "even if we, or an angel from heaven, should preach to you a gospel contrary to what we have preached to you, he is to be accursed!" (Galatians 1:8). The same apostle said that "Satan disguises himself as an angel of light" (2 Corinthians 11:14), thus warning believers to be careful that the gospel they embrace is consistent with the content of the gospel as preached by the apostles themselves. Innovations may be useful, but there is no room for innovation in the message of the evangel.

A NEW FAITH?

By 1520, three short years after Luther had nailed his famous Ninety-five Theses to the university church door in Wittenberg, he had become the best-known man in all of Germany. His following came from several circles within the society of the time.

All who opposed the church for any reason applauded him because of his boldness in attacking the Catholic Church. Scholars saw in him a man who could help break the chains of intellectual oppression in the universities. German nationalists saw in him a leader pointing the way to political liberty. The peasants rallied to him as a deliverer who would help them find economic freedom. Sadly, only a few saw his real concern—the theology of the church at that time. Some who did understand were Nicholas Amsdorf, John Brenz, and Philip Melanchthon. These, with various nonscholars here and there, were drawn to his writings and preaching precisely because of his insight into the gospel.

As we saw in chapter 3, Luther's primary concern was centered in the gospel message of justification by faith alone. This was not a novel idea—it was the teaching of Romans 4:5 and Galatians 3:22. It had never entirely disappeared from the historic church, but Luther was to give it new meaning by making it the primary article of the church, the *defining principle* of the Christian life. Here faith would grow, assurance would be solidified, and saints would flourish in faith and hope.

In Luther's theology, justification is seen as a definitive act of God. It is a grace given to sinners for the sake of Christ, whereby He forgives people all their sin and counts them entirely righteous. He grants this pardon on the basis of their receiving the free gift of eternal life in Christ alone. Justification must not be confused with sanctification, an act wherein a process begins and continues. In sanctification, which is always present when a person is justified, God makes people progressively more holy. Thus, a person might be partially sanctified. This, indeed, is always the case, because even the most godly are, as Luther put it, simultaneously sinful yet justified and thus in need of continual sanctifying grace.

But here is the critical point—in justification there can be no room for growth. There is no partial, progressive, or continuing justification going on inside the life of a believer in Christ. A person is either entirely justified or he is not. And justification comes to sinful people on the basis of God's kindness and goodness alone. It is a gift God bestows, not a status a person achieves.

The word *merit* can, therefore, have absolutely no place in this matter. And this struck at the very heart of what had developed in the Middle Ages (see chapter 2).

God is holy. He cannot allow sinful creatures into fellowship with Himself. All the confession in the world will not ultimately make a sinner anything other than a sinner. Luther understood this. His deep preoccupation with his own sin almost drove him insane. Because of this, countless psychotherapeutic writers have attacked him as a neurotic and semideranged person. What he was, in the best medieval sense, was a man who believed explicitly the teaching of his church regarding the fear of God, His awesome power, and His determination to judge sin.

What Luther came to understand in 1517 and beyond was that God was also gracious. He had provided satisfaction for mankind's offense against Himself in the death of Christ. Here salvation is freely provided. In the gospel an announcement is given and an offer is made. This is grace—not some magical power that pours grace into hearts through sacraments. God grants grace to sinners, but they must accept it. This is faith—trusting in God for Christ's sake, or, simply put, entrusting all that I am as a sinner to all that Christ is as a Savior.

It is not bare acknowledgment or creedal affirmation. It is leaning oneself entirely upon the person and work of Jesus as offered in the gospel. Faith is relationship—trust by me, a person, in Christ, a person who redeems me. It is all based solely on the grace of God. When I believe the gospel, I am counted (credited, reckoned) as righteous immediately. God gives me His Spirit, by which I am empowered to begin, for the first time ever, to do works that God will find acceptable because of Christ.

A NEW AUTHORITY?

For this faith to be born in people, the promises of God are needed. These promises are the gospel of grace. They come through the Scriptures, especially as they are properly preached. For Luther all of Scripture consists of law and gospel. Both are the Word of God. Through the law people come to know the will of God and His stern, righteous, holy demands. From the same Scriptures people learn of the gospel, the free grace of a benevolent God who will forgive.

The Scriptures are God's Word because here He speaks. They are given by the inspiration of the Holy Spirit (literally, "breathed out by the Spirit"). This means that the resulting text of the written word is exactly and infallibly what God intended. The personalities of human authors can be seen in the written Scriptures, but the result of their writing is God's Word!

What Luther claimed for the Scriptures is still important today. He believed that God continued to speak to men and women, but only through the Scriptures. Indeed, only through the Scriptures does God come to people with His truth and clearly reveal Himself. He does not reveal Himself through church organizations, special mystical revelations, ecstatic visions, or apparitions. The only *authority* the visible church has is that of the Scriptures. If it departs from the Word of God, it is a blind guide and will fall into the ditch, taking many others with it. Further, the Scriptures will not yield correct interpretation except to a person of faith. Rationalistic, humanistic wisdom will serve no salvific purpose when it comes to handling the Scriptures.

When the Scriptures come to a person as a sinner, they rouse his sleeping conscience via the law and its demands. He is convicted of sin, righteousness, and judgment to come, as Jesus taught. He then must flee to the promises of the gospel. The law cannot help him one iota. When the sinner has believed the gospel, he then sees the law in a new way, as a guide for his conduct because of the gospel. The law will never conquer sin within the believer, but it will repeatedly inform him regarding proper thought and conduct, and it drives him back to the gospel day after day. Here he finds safety.

But What About the Church?

From this it stands to reason that the church cannot be the institution that mediates salvation to the souls of people. The church is to be understood, primarily, as a "communion of saints," or a spiritual fellowship of all who believe the gospel and are justified. What the visible church can, and must, do is to bring men and women to the Word of God. It does this in two ways—through preaching and through the sacraments.

In its preaching it declares both law and gospel. In the sacraments (literally, "sacred signs") it declares God's promises with the signs given by Christ. Protestant Reformers disagreed regarding the nature of these signs, but all agreed that there were only two clearly delineated in the Scriptures. Rome believed then, and still does, that there are seven (see chapter 6).

The Reformers believed that the Word was effective. Wherever it was preached in faith it would have a powerful effect in bringing God's elect to eternal life. And where this Word gathers a people who believe the gospel, you have a visible church after the pattern of the New Testament. This meant that the church did not need a continuation of bishops or a constant form of ecclesiastical government to form an organized body truly faithful to the New Testament. Indeed, the church is free under the Word of God to organize itself as an assembly of believers with gospel ministers. Those believers who form such a church are free to set up or depose teachers as they see fit when guided by the Word of God.

These are essentially the great truths recovered and plainly taught by the Protestants of the sixteenth century. Their consistent application breaks down the Roman synthesis of the Middle Ages. These principles attack the very foundation of the papacy, the magisterium (the official teaching authority of the church), and the sacramental system of Rome. But why?

The grace of God cannot be mediated by the church through her rule over the souls of people and, at the same time, by the Word of God alone. If the disputants of the sixteenth century were anything, and this was true on both sides, they were logically consistent. They both believed in the law of noncontradiction. Two mutually exclusive claims cannot both be true at the same time. Both might be wrong, but if one is correct the other must be wrong.

Luther's approach attacked the apparatus of ritualism. It set up the preaching of the Word of God and the proper administration of the two warranted sacraments as the sole function of the church. (Calvin later added, properly upon careful biblical reflection, the so-called "third mark" of the visible church—discipline.)

Luther and the Reformers were not radicals in terms of how they viewed history. They believed that however corrupt the church had become it had done so under God's sovereign purpose. God had permitted this course for a purpose, even if it was to punish sin in its leaders. What history has revealed should not be discarded lightly and flippantly. If what we see around us is contrary to the revealed will of God, then it must be abolished, but to totally tear down the church was never their desire. They worked to retain all that they could and to conserve the heritage of the past. They frequently appealed to the writings of the church Fathers. They read and understood the theologians of the Middle Ages. This was especially true for Luther. But what kept the Catholic Church from embracing these theological distinctives of the Reformation?

THE COUNTER-REFORMATION
AND THE COUNCIL OF TRENT

Rome sought to correct its acknowledged abuses in the whole matter of indulgences and immoral practice by launching a reformation movement of its own in 1523. Pope Hadrian VI acknowledged that the church needed a thorough reformation, which would begin at Rome itself. Unfortunately he died before he could begin this effort, and his successor, Clement VII (1523–1534), was chosen partly on his expressed opposition to this reforming effort.

During the next ten years efforts to reform the church continued from within. New societies of priests were formed, as had been previously the case over the centuries. Charles V pressed the church for a general council to discuss theological matters. In 1536 these two lines of thought formed a consensus that resulted in changes both at Rome itself and later in the church at large. Pope Pius III appointed to the college of cardinals "reform-minded" men, and from their number eventually came three reforming popes in the decades that followed.

During this time the call for a general papal council grew stronger and stronger. This council was finally convened in 1545, just months before Luther's death in February of 1546. This council met at the city of Trent on three occasions, finally finishing its work in 1563. It had three purposes in its meetings, all stated in a papal bull (document). First, it sought to define Catholic doctrine more clearly, especially as over against the doctrine of the Protestants. Second, it worked toward the reformation of church life. Third, it purposed to clarify present heresies and drive them out of the church of Rome completely.

The doctrines adopted by the council were essentially restatements of the doctrinal positions of the later Middle Ages. These were the very teachings that the Protestant Reformers had struggled against. The council clearly had the writings of Luther and Calvin in mind, if not actually in hand, and what was written repudiated the essential doctrinal tenets of the Protestant efforts.

The decrees relating to church reform dealt also with matters raised by the Protestants. They urged greater pastoral care for the laity and more effective preaching by priests. The whole oversight of the bishops over dioceses was strengthened practically. Some decrees of the council addressed the need for real reformation in papal practices, but the council was not unified on this matter. The question of the supremacy of the pope over the whole church, which was and is a stumbling block for many, was also treated, but no clear decision was reached.

Even as the council met between 1545 and 1563 there was a glimmer of hope that the Roman Church would plainly embrace the gospel of grace. Some cardinals in the church did see truth in the concern of the Reformers. The rejection of the gospel by the pope was not yet solidified in these days. Michael Horton correctly sums up the situation:

> The door was open to the full reformation of Western Christendom until the Council of Trent . . . finally closed it with its devastating

canons against the gospel. Things that had been left to debate in the universities were now closed to discussion as the Council issued what it considered infallible pronouncements on the doctrine of justification and related truths. Now, issues upon which men and women of goodwill could differ were given a single answer: tradition is equal to Scripture in authority; the interpretation of Scripture and the elements of Holy Communion are to be denied to the laity; the Mass is a repetition of Christ's sacrifice and each Mass atones for the people; transubstantiation was officially affirmed, as was belief in purgatory. (Armstrong, 256)

All this is very sad because it left the church deeply divided. What is even sadder, however, was the longest decree of the whole Council—the one titled *Concerning Justification*. The early portions of this decree are agreeable to both Reformers and Catholics. They attack the major errors cited by Augustine against Pelagius in the early controversies of the church. But right within this portion comes this line: "they who by sin had been cut off from God may be disposed through his quickening and helping grace to convert themselves to their own justification by freely assenting to and cooperating with that grace." A person cannot, said the document, "by his own free will and without the grace of God" move himself toward justice in the sight of God, yet he can and must cooperate with grace in the end.

What follows is a definition that is crucial to understanding the great divide. The Council defined *justification* as "not only a remission of sins but also the sanctification and renewal of the inward man through the voluntary reception of grace and gifts whereby an unjust man becomes just." This is in clear contradiction to Luther's teaching and that of other Protestants who insisted, with the apostle Paul, that justification and sanctification are not one and the same. Sanctification should not be denied, but the renewal of the inward believer is not the same thing as justification. *Justification is a once-and-for-all act.*

In justification we move immediately, on the basis of faith alone, from being unjust, condemned, lost, and without hope into a position of being just, acquitted, saved, and filled with true hope! In contrast to this, the Council of Trent said that God puts His

Spirit within us in order to renew us and move us progressively from being unjust to being just. This is a *process,* albeit one begun and ostensibly carried out by grace, but nonetheless a process. But that is not what is being taught in Romans 4:1–5, where the apostle says that justification comes to those who are wicked, who stop trying to work for it, and who therefore accept it by faith. Paul's clear point is this: God justifies the sinner *as a sinner,* not on the basis of anything done in the flesh. This is good news—gospel!

If this sounds like an overstating of the differences between the Reformers' understanding of justification and that of the Catholic Church, listen to the strong language of several of the canons of the decree on justification from the Council of Trent:

> Canon 9. If anyone says that the sinner is justified by faith alone . . . , meaning that nothing else is required to cooperate in order to obtain the grace of justification, and that it is not in any way necessary that he be prepared and disposed by the action of his own will, let him be anathema.
>
> . . . .
>
> Canon 11. If anyone says that men are justified either by the sole imputation of the justice of Christ or by the sole remission of sins, to the exclusion of the grace and charity which is poured forth in their hearts by the Holy Ghost (Romans 5:5), and remains in them, or also that the grace by which we are justified is only the good will of God, let him be anathema.
>
> Canon 12. If anyone says that justifying faith is nothing else than confidence in divine mercy . . . , which remits sins for Christ's sake, or that it is this confidence alone that justifies us, let him be anathema.
>
> . . . .
>
> Canon 24. If anyone says that the justice received is not preserved and also not increased before God through good works . . . , but that those works are merely the fruits and signs of justification obtained, but not the cause of the increase, let him be anathema.
>
> . . . .
>
> Canon 30. If anyone says that after the reception of the grace of justification the guilt is so remitted and the debt of eternal punishment so blotted out to every repentant sinner, that no debt of temporal punishment remains to be discharged either in this world or in purgatory before the gates of heaven can be opened, let him be anathema.

. . . .

Canon 32. If anyone says that the good works of the one justified are in such manner the gifts of God that they are not also the good merits of him justified; or that the one justified by the good works that he performs by the grace of God and the merit of Jesus Christ, whose living member he is, does not truly merit an increase of grace, eternal life, and in case he dies in grace the attainment of eternal life itself and also an increase of glory, let him be anathema.

SUMMING UP

What all this plainly affirms is that, according to the Council of Trent, sinners are made right with God over the course of their entire lives (and beyond) on the basis of their cooperating with God's grace in the inner work of the Holy Spirit rather than on the basis of the finished work of Christ on the cross. Surely there is no room for any remaining doubt when we conclude, in the spirit of gentleness, that the answer given to the vital question "What must I do to be saved?" has two radically different answers. One answer is that confessed by the Reformers (and evangelicals since), and the other is that confessed by the Council of Trent (and the Catholic Church since).

What happened at Trent may not be irreversible. God alone knows. What is obviously true is this—no Catholic council or creed since Trent has fundamentally altered either the language or the theology of this important sixteenth-century decision. A door was closed by that Council, a door that many of us pray might someday be opened.

PART TWO

THE THEOLOGICAL ISSUES

The Protestant Reformation originally set out to address several abuses in the church, but before three years passed the deeper issues surfaced in the midst of a major debate. These issues were not easily correctable by moral and social changes initiated by Rome.

By the 1520s the central issues of the debate revolved around two major doctrinal points. These two points were known as the formal and material principles of the Reformation. The formal principle, or that which formed the Reformation, was the doctrine of Scripture. What is authority? Where is it found? In the church or in the Bible alone? Is written Scripture sufficient for all faith and practice? What is the place of tradition, of the teaching authority of the pope and the church? How should we respond to councils, creeds, and confessions if they conflict with the written Word? Is the central teaching of Scripture clear?

The material principle was equally important to the formal. In this the Protestant Reformers followed Paul's teaching in Romans that people are made right with God by Christ alone, through grace alone. The key part of this equation was that Christ and grace were received by faith alone. By this the Reformers stressed that true faith laid hold of Christ and the grace of God without any human merit.

These two principles exposed a number of serious theological differences with Rome that are still the cause of division today.

CHAPTER FIVE

THE CENTRAL MYSTERY OF THE CHRISTIAN FAITH?

For centuries the central mystery and feature of Roman Catholic worship and practice has been the Mass. Most Catholics know more about the Mass than almost any other aspect of their faith. Few evangelicals understand Catholic dogma at this central point. What exactly is the Mass? What happens in the Mass according to Catholic dogma? Where and how did this practice actually begin? And, most importantly, what does the New Testament say about the Lord's Supper?

THE ROMAN CATHOLIC DOCTRINE OF THE MASS

When you talk to any three or four different Catholics, you will often find various views of the Mass. The same can be said of Protestants. Ask any three or four of them what happens in their church when the Lord's Supper, or Communion, is taken. The answers will vary widely. Confusion abounds in our respective groups. It is best, therefore, that we not get a definition of the Mass from the "street" but from official sources and statements. It is important that evangelicals not misrepresent Catholic dogma regarding the Mass.

For years a standard catechism used by Catholics in training communicants was the book called *A Catechism of Christian Doctrine*. It says, "The Holy Mass is one and the same with that of the Cross, inasmuch as Christ, who offered Himself, a bleeding victim, on the Cross to His Heavenly father, continues to offer Himself in an unbloody manner on the altar, through the ministry of

His priests" (p. 47). This definition is consistent with older Catholic teaching clearly set forth by the Council of Trent (1545–1563). There really isn't much room to misunderstand the doctrine's implications when the words of the "Canons on the Sacrifice of the Mass" are read carefully:

> Canon 1. If anyone says that in the mass a true and real sacrifice is not offered to God; or that to be offered is nothing else than that Christ is given to us to eat, let him be anathema.
> Canon 2. If anyone says by those words "Do this for a commemoration of me," Christ did not institute the Apostles priests, or did not ordain that they and other priests should offer his own body and blood, let him be anathema.
> Canon 3. If anyone says that the sacrifice of the mass is one and only of praise and thanksgiving; or that it is a mere commemoration of the sacrifice consummated on the cross and not a propitiatory one, let him be anathema.

The title of chapter 2 of the "Doctrine Concerning the Sacrifice of the Mass" (from the Twenty-Second Session, 17 September 1562) is "The Sacrifice of the Mass is Propitiatory Both for the Living and the Dead." This section says,

> And inasmuch as this divine sacrifice which is celebrated in the Mass is contained and immolated [offered] in an unbloody manner the same Christ who once offered Himself in a bloody manner on the altar of the cross, the holy council teaches that this is truly propitiatory and has this effect, that if we, contrite and penitent, with sincere heart and upright faith, with fear and reverence, draw nigh to God, we obtain mercy and find grace in seasonable aid (Heb. 4:16).

Interestingly chapter 8 says that the Mass may not be celebrated in the vernacular tongue, though its mysteries should be explained to the common people. This teaching was plainly altered by Vatican II (1962–1965).

Modern Catholic thought on these matters has changed only very slightly from what we read above. The *Catechism of the Catholic Church* states, "The holy Eucharist completes Christian initiation. Those who have been raised to the dignity of the royal priesthood by Baptism and configured more deeply to Christ by

Confirmation participate with the whole community in the Lord's own sacrifice by means of the Eucharist" (Ratzinger, 334). This same modern Catechism then adds,

> The Eucharist is "the source and summit of the Christian life." "The other sacraments, and indeed all ecclesiastical ministries and works of the apostolate, are bound up with the Eucharist and are oriented toward it. For in the blessed Eucharist is contained the whole spiritual good of the Church, namely Christ himself, our Pasch [Paschal Lamb]."

The Mass is said to be "the sum and substance of our faith" a few sentences later (Ratzinger, 334).

It is imperative that the evangelical understand that without the Mass your Catholic friend has no religion, no faith to practice, and no communion and fellowship with Christ. It is for the discerning Catholic both a sacrament and a sacrifice. It is a sacrament because the worshiper is nourished by the body and blood of Christ —Christ is actually received by the Catholic worshiper. It is a sacrifice because a gift is offered to God. Christ is offered by the priest, on behalf of the congregation, to God the Father.

Does Catholic theology see the Mass as a separate sacrifice from that of the cross, as some Protestants have written? No. What is actually taught is that the sacrifice of Calvary is one and the same as the sacrifice of the Mass. It is believed that the same victim and the same offering as that of Calvary is sacramentally, mysteriously, present on the altar of the Mass. Christ, in the Mass, "continues to offer Himself in an unbloody manner, by the hands of His priests on our altars" (*Catechism of the Synod of Maynooth*, 51).

Thus, Roman Catholic dogma denies that the Mass is simply a dramatic reenactment or commemoration of Christ's death. It is a real sacrifice that continues the eternal sacrifice of Christ, which is above time. Contemporary Catholic apologist Karl Keating says, "Although Christ died only once, through the Mass his saving act is made actually present, day by day, until the end of the world" (Keating, 53).

The faithful Catholic must take the Mass at least once a year. He must be in a state of grace when he takes the Mass; that is, without unconfessed mortal sin. Many modern American Catholics must think that they rarely commit a mortal sin, since the practice of confession has declined in recent years. In this, American Catholics are fundamentally wrong according to the dogma of their own church.

For a sin to be mortal, three requirements must be met. Writes Keating, "First, it must be a serious matter. Second, there must be sufficient reflection on its seriousness. And, third, there must be full consent in the committing of it" (Keating, 66). What exactly is a "serious matter"? Any sin contrary to the Ten Commandments or the moral teaching of the church can qualify: murder, adultery, envy, abortion, artificial birth control, thievery, sodomy, fornication, stealing, and lying all fit the category.

Finally, one of the most important and distinctive elements of the Roman Catholic doctrine of the Mass is what is called transubstantiation. In this teaching it is believed that the bread and wine in the Mass are converted (changed) into the body and blood of Christ Himself. The whole substance of the bread and wine is converted into the whole substance of Christ's body, but without the appearance changing. The bread still looks like bread and tastes like bread, but it is really, fundamentally, actually, the flesh of Jesus. This teaching has ancient roots, but it goes beyond the Scriptures' plain teaching.

The Mass is more than an evangelical eucharist ("thanksgiving") or the Lord's Supper, wherein we nurture faith by the elements that point us to Christ and strengthen our faith in Him. It is the supreme moment in the entire worship of the church. This is the time when the priest offers Christ as a sacrifice for the living and the dead. In this sense Christ is on the altar, offered up before God the Father and the people in a sacrifice continuous with Calvary. That is why Catholics bow, venerate, and adore the host (Latin, "victim") in the Mass. They believe they are showing reverence to Christ Himself.

When Catholics take the host they sincerely believe that they eat the body of Jesus Christ, which is *indispensable* for their salvation. That is also why the priest raises the host before the flock and declares, "This is the Lamb of God who takes away the sin of the world."

THE ORIGINS OF THE MASS

Paul Johnson, a noted British historian and Roman Catholic churchman, has written a most interesting and useful book titled *The History of Christianity*. In his treatment he looks at how Christianity changed to meet the public opinion of the first four centuries. He writes that the church "in the second century . . . had acquired the elements of ecclesiastical organization; in the third it created an intellectual and philosophical structure; and in the fourth, especially in the later half of the century, it built up a dramatic and impressive public persona: it began to think and act like a state Church" (Johnson, 99).

As the dress of the nobleman became the dress of bishops, reactions came from both those who favored change and those who opposed it. The church began to take on forms and practices that were beyond its simple and humble origins in first-century Jewish culture. In addition, new practices were adopted and doctrines developed that explained or defended and defined these practices. Some of these changes might well have been harmless and even useful to some extent. But the problem is that the church has always had the tendency to adopt the pattern of the world, of other religions, or of state governments and political forces.

With the Mass a doctrine evolved that explained the mysteries now accepted as biblical by Catholics. Johnson is again helpful:

> The basic framework of the mass had already existed in the mid-second century, when it was described by Justin Martyr. It consisted of readings from the memoirs of the apostles and the Old Testament; a sermon; a prayer followed by the kiss of peace and the distribution of the blessed bread and water. This Sunday eucharist had become an absolute obligation by Justin's time and the words of the central prayer became formalized in the next generation or two. . . . The effect . . . was to change an essentially simple ceremony into a much lengthier and more formal one, involving an element of grandeur. . . . Some of the ceremonial aspects were taken over from pagan rites, others from court practice, which became far more elaborate after the transfer to

Constantinople. . . . The object was to replace the magnificence of pagan ritual in the public mind, also partly to win the struggle against Arianism. . . . At the end of the fourth century John Chrysostom spoke of the Lord's table as "a place of terror and shuddering," not to be seen by profane eyes, and it became customary to screen it with curtains . . . , whose effect was to hide all the operations on the altar from the congregation as a whole, and to deepen the chasm between clergy and laity. (Johnson, 101–2)

As early as the second and third century the Mass began to be referred to by some church theologians as a sacrifice. Some spoke of it as the commemoration of Christ's passion, while others began to write of it as an actual offering in reparation for sins. By the Middle Ages the church, having borrowed both philosophically and religiously from numerous sources, could speak of the Mass at the Council of Trent as a bloodless sacrifice. In 1215, after three centuries of often intense debate, the church at the Lateran Council accepted the idea that during the Mass the bread and wine become the body and blood of Christ (transubstantiation).

In ancient ritual blood sacrifices (in pagan religions) the worshiper must consume the blood of the victim as a sacrifice. This idea was incorporated in such a manner that now the communing believer takes the bread (the body of Christ) into his own flesh in this the supreme and highest moment of Christian worship. This becomes the central mystery of the Christian's faith and practice—eating the body of Christ.

The Mass was enshrined in an elaborate ritual, in time, much like a "rare gem in a costly setting," as one historian puts it. When the priest spoke the appointed words over the bread and wine a miracle took place. The miracle was transubstantiation. The broken body and outpoured blood are offered up to God as a sacrifice for the living and the dead. The liturgy reaches its apex when the "host" (the consecrated wafer, now Christ's body) is lifted high in the air, and the Mass bell rung. Here the worshiper prostrates himself in humility before the physically present Savior, Christ Jesus Himself. In past ages, where superstition abounded, miracles were frequently associated with these moments in the Mass. In

my visits to Latin America I have seen this same kind of pheno-
menon claimed in our age.

As noted earlier, until Vatican II the Mass was not said in the
language of the people. The priest did not face the congregation,
and usually the cup was not given to the communicants, since the
bread was the body of Christ itself. Much of this has changed
since 1965. What has not changed is the fundamental nature of the
Mass as a sacrifice in which Christ is believed to be really present
in the bread and wine. True and devout Catholics still believe that
Christ is physically present in the bread and wine. This teaching,
therefore, has powerful influence over the whole perception of
what constitutes acceptable Christian worship.

THE TEACHING OF THE NEW TESTAMENT

An appeal to the New Testament is often not enough for the
Roman Catholic. Why is this so? Because the magisterium of the
church is his final authority in matters of faith and practice. We
simply cannot escape the delineating character of "Scripture
alone" no matter how much we seek to understand one another
and explain our differences. We do have two entirely different au-
thorities for our faith and practice. And nothing underscores this
problem more than the doctrine and practice of the Mass.

What do I mean by the magisterium? This is the church's teaching authority. It is believed that this authority was instituted by
Christ Himself and that it has been guided by the Holy Spirit. Its
task is to safeguard the truth and explain and interpret it properly
for the faithful. It is exercised in two ways: *extraordinary*—popes
and councils infallibly define truth or morals that are necessary for
one's salvation and that have been constantly taught and held by
the church over the ages; *ordinary*—the church infallibly defines
the truths of the faith. These must be truths that are (1) taught
universally and without dissent, (2) taught or the magisterium
would be failing in its duty, (3) connected with a grave matter of
faith or morals, and (4) taught authoritatively. Not everything
taught by the magisterium is done so infallibly; however, it is believed that the exercise of the magisterium is faithful to Christ and

what He taught, as defined in Our Sunday Visitor's *Catholic Dictionary.*

When the Protestant Reformers protested the practices of the sixteenth-century church, they made much out of the need for a complete doctrinal and practical reform in public worship. John Calvin, the great Swiss Reformer, believed that the church's worship had become "gross idolatry" by the Middle Ages and that this needed just as much attention in the cause of true reformation as the doctrine of justification by faith. Calvin wished to replace what he called a "godly show" with a simple, radically biblical, public service of worship that was developed according to the revealed patterns of the New Testament Scriptures.

Robert Godfrey, a historian of the Protestant Reformation, sums up the concern of men like Calvin:

> Calvin laments that the simplicity of sacramental doctrine and practice that prevailed in the early church has been lost. This is most clearly seen in the Lord's Supper. Eucharistic sacrifice, transubstantiation, and the worship of the consecrated bread and wine are unbiblical and destroy the real meaning of the sacrament. "While the sacrament ought to have been a means of raising pious minds to heaven, the sacred symbols of the Supper were abused to an entirely different purpose, and men, contented with gazing upon them and worshipping them, never once thought of Christ." The work of Christ is destroyed, as can be seen in the idea of eucharistic sacrifice, where "Christ was sacrificed a thousand times a-day, as if he had not done enough in once dying for us." (Armstrong, 73)

For Calvin, who developed a biblical theology of the Lord's Supper that carefully followed the text of the New Testament, the elements did not become the actual body and blood of Christ physically, nor was Christ sacrificed on the altar for the people. Rather, true believers, when they came to communion, ate and drank in faith, believing that Christ was present with them in the fellowship of His appointed meal. He could not be seen, for His body was physically in heaven, but His Spirit was there in the fellowship of His people communing with them through the visible signs of the sacrament. This seems, quite simply, to be the correct rendering of the meaning of 1 Corinthians 10:16 and 11:17–34, the two critical apostolic texts on the Lord's Supper that exist outside the institution of the meal by our Lord (see Matthew 26:20–29; Mark 14:22–25; Luke 22:14–23).

Think for a moment about our Lord's institution of the Supper as recorded in Matthew 26:26–29. First, Jesus takes bread and wine, saying that these were His body and blood. Did any of those present have any such idea as transubstantiation? Would not they have heard His words exactly like we would read them in the text? Jesus was standing in their very presence. He had not even died yet! They heard Him say after they had drunk the wine, "I will not drink of this fruit of the vine from now on . . ." (v. 29). He did not say, "I will not drink my blood . . . ." If only the appearance of wine remained but the reality was now blood, why would we expect Him not to say this?

In teaching that the "substance" changes in the elements of the Mass, while the outward "accidents" do not, Rome falls into serious contradiction. Is not the inward nature of the object that which truly produces the outward appearance? Further, where in Scripture is there a miracle where the outward appearance remains unchanged but those who observe the miracle are expected to believe that a real miracle has actually taken place? To suggest that God deals with mankind in this manner raises serious problems.

When we read the gospel passages about the actual institution of the Lord's Supper, we plainly discover that the language is figurative. The teaching of Jesus on that last evening with His disciples is given in fullest measure in John 13–17. Here, throughout the entire evening, we discover that figures of speech abound. Further, the apostles were Jews, and Jews had strict dietary laws—laws that clearly prohibited their eating foods that contained blood (see Acts 15:28–29). Years after the Lord had instituted this special meal, Peter says, "I have never eaten anything unholy and unclean" (10:14). If he had been eating and drinking the body and blood of Christ for several years, how could he have said this?

Jesus had promised to be with His own throughout the ages

(see John 14:16–18). He was going to send the Holy Spirit who would make Him known to them. Christ's presence is not in buildings or even in rituals. He is with His people when they do what He commands. He is blessing them, revealing His presence to them, when they keep His commandments. His two signs (visible commandments), given to His gathered people, are baptism and the Lord's Supper. When we eat and drink in remembrance of Him, He is there, but not *physically* in the bread and wine. He is there by the Holy Spirit, strengthening the faith of His people as they commune with Him in obedience.

If Holy Communion is not a real sacrifice or the eating of the real body of Christ, what is it? In 1 Corinthians 10:21 Paul calls the cup "the cup of the Lord." He speaks of our drinking as "a sharing in" (*koinonia*, "fellowship"; v. 16) with the Lord. In 11:17–34 the apostle teaches, further, that in this meal God's people gather to remember the greatest display of love ever given to them. As a result of this powerful remembrance of Christ they are to love one another, something that in Corinth they were not doing very well. As a spiritual family they were to gather at this table to celebrate Christ's grace and mercy for them and to be united in love for Him and each other. Here they were to remember Him "until He comes." This is the meaning of the meal that Christ gave to His church. No amount of tradition should be allowed to tamper with the simple truths plainly set forth in the text of Scripture itself.

If you are a practicing Catholic and consider yourself to also be a person of evangelical faith in Christ, you must consider your faith in the light of the plain Catholic dogma of the Mass. Your church requires you to be in agreement with this doctrine, if you continue to receive the Mass week by week. You are to say an "Amen" when the priest says, "The body of Christ." This "Amen" is a solemn Hebrew word that means "It is so, this is the body of Christ!" The church requires you to refrain from taking the communion if you do not agree with her. You cannot escape the force of Scripture upon your own conscience. You must decide this utterly serious matter before God and His Word.

CHAPTER SIX

SEVEN
SACRAMENTS?

A s we saw in earlier chapters Roman Catholicism has seven sacraments. Evangelicals have only two—baptism and communion. Both the number of sacraments and the definition, or nature, of each is a subject that displays deep differences between evangelical Christians and Roman Catholics. In this chapter we will look at the Roman Catholic definition of a sacrament, why the church teaches that there are seven, and what each sacrament means to the faith of the devout Catholic.

INTRODUCTION

As with the Mass, the six other sacraments in Catholic practice hinge ultimately upon the doctrine of the authority of the church. Scripture is appealed to in the definition of each of the seven sacraments, but the church's historically evolving understanding of each came to fruition in a past council or in a papal decision that ultimately defined what the Catholic understanding of a particular sacrament is. In other words, it is believed that the seed for the practice is in Scripture, but the flower will come to bloom through the work of the magisterium. In Catholic doctrine the understanding develops and "the acorn becomes a tree" in the development of dogma. This observation is plainly stated in the new *Catechism of the Catholic Church*: "As she has done for the canon of Sacred Scripture and for the doctrine of the faith, the Church, by the power of the Spirit who guides her 'into all truth,' has gradually recognized this treasure . . . and has determined its 'dispensation'" (Ratzinger, 289–90).

When evangelicals are drawn to Catholicism, or when Catholics consider their own faith and practice in the light of evangelical beliefs, certain factors become powerfully attractive. For this reason we cannot respond to the matter of the sacraments simply by appealing to history and to the creeds. We need to understand the actual doctrine, as Catholicism teaches it, asking at each point, "What is the biblical warrant for this teaching?"

WHAT IS A SACRAMENT?

Sacraments are defining characteristics for Roman Catholicism. In sacramental religion, grace comes to the soul not directly but in a mediated manner. The evangelical generally thinks in terms of God coming to him directly by the ministry of the Holy Spirit *through* the Word of God. The Catholic thinks of God coming to him through the sacramental ministry of the church. He comes particularly through the seven sacraments.

Salvation is understood, in Catholic thought, in terms of the descent of a higher reality. Catholic teaching clearly has a place for the merit of Christ atoning for human sin, but when this teaching is mixed with the mystical notions of the Catholic faith in the context of sacramental life, something higher, or deeper, than the historical death of Christ is what saves. In the sacraments God actually comes down and lifts up the sinner, who then takes His grace. This makes him a partaker of the divine nature through the life of the church.

But what exactly is a sacrament? According to the Council of Trent, a sacrament is an "effective sign of grace instituted by Christ." The new *Catechism of the Catholic Church* maintains the same centuries-old teaching: "The whole liturgical life of the Church revolves around the Eucharistic sacrifice and the sacraments"; and, further, "Jesus' words and actions during his hidden life and public ministry were already salvific. . . . They announced and prepared what he was going to give the Church when all was accomplished. The mysteries of Christ's life are the foundations of what he would henceforth dispense in the sacraments" (Ratzinger, 289).

It is also imperative that we understand the power and saving role these sacraments have in the life of the Christian. Most evangelicals who discuss this with Catholics have little idea of the teaching of the Roman Church on this matter. The *Catechism of the Catholic Church* adds, "Celebrated worthily in faith, the sacraments confer the grace that they signify. They are *efficacious* because in them Christ himself is at work: it is he who baptizes, he who acts in his sacraments in order to communicate the grace that each sacrament signifies" (Ratzinger, 292).

All this is understood by the faithful Catholic to mean that the sacrament is more than a sign that declares, or points to, the reality. It *is* the reality; it actually effects in the heart of baptized believers something of God's grace. This is the whole idea behind the argument surrounding the Latin phrase *ex opere operato*—that is, by virtue of the performance of the act grace is actually given.

The essentials of any Catholic sacrament, by definition, are three. There is, first, the *matter*. This refers to the physical substance itself (in the case of penance or marriage the *action* perceived by the human senses is the matter). Second, there is the *form*. This refers to the words employed, which are determined by the church and are not to be altered. Finally, there is a minister with the right *intention*. Where these essentials are present you have, according to Catholic teaching, a valid sacrament.

Newer Catholic teaching, in distinction from the Council of Trent, seems more intent on saying that faith must reside in the one who receives the sacrament or it is not effective. The argument is that sacraments presuppose faith in some sense, but in words and objects they are still said to nourish, strengthen, and express faith mystically. This is a major improvement, but the evangelical still must be troubled by the idea of a sacrament effecting what it represents. How can grace actually be imparted via a sacrament?

Take baptism as a significant example. The Catholic doctrine is this: Baptism not only represents the cleansing of the soul from sin, but it actually effects the cleansing in the action of the sacrament. Says the *Catechism of the Catholic Church,* "Baptism not only purifies from all sins, but also makes the neophyte 'a new creature,' an adopted son of God, who has become a 'partaker of the divine nature,' member of Christ and co-heir with him, and a temple of the Holy Spirit" (Ratzinger, 322). Very simply, baptism *conveys* the actual grace and saves the person who receives it. He is made a child of God in the action of the baptism. The *Catechism* adds, "Baptism makes us members of the Body of Christ. . . . From the baptismal font is born the one People of God" (Ratzinger, 322).

Because of such teaching, the earlier reference to the phrase *ex opere operato* is not out of line. Indeed, the same *Catechism of the Catholic Church* summarizes the church's sacramental teaching:

> Celebrated worthily in faith, the sacraments confer the grace that they signify. They are efficacious because in them Christ himself is at work: it is he who baptizes, he who acts in the sacraments in order to communicate the grace that each sacrament signifies. The Father always hears the prayer of the Son's Church which, in the [divine calling] of each sacrament, expresses her faith in the power of the Spirit. As fire transforms into itself everything it touches, so the Holy Spirit transforms into the divine life whatever is subjected to his power. This is the meaning of the Church's affirmation that the sacraments act *ex opere operato* (literally "by the very fact of the action's being performed"), i.e., by virtue of the saving work of Christ, accomplished once for all. It follows that "the sacrament is not wrought by the righteousness of either the celebrant or the recipient, but by the power of God. From the moment a sacrament is celebrated in accordance with the intention of the Church, the power of Christ and his Spirit acts in and through it, independently of the personal holiness of the minister. Nevertheless, the fruits of the sacraments also depend on the disposition of the one who receives them. (Ratzinger, 292)

So sacraments "confer grace." They are "efficacious." By analogy, as fire transforms everything it touches, so the Spirit uses sacraments to transform all that the sacraments touch, and, in the aforementioned sense, this is *ex opere operato;* that is, the thing is actually accomplished by the sacrament.

WHAT ARE THE SEVEN SACRAMENTS?

Roman Catholic theology teaches that the number of sacraments is seven, not two as taught by historic evangelical theology. What are these seven sacraments, and how does Catholic theology define them? Each definition that follows is paraphrased from the book Our Sunday Visitor's *Catholic Encyclopedia*. The intention is to properly represent official understanding of the Catholic position.

1. *Baptism.* The sacrament in which the one baptized is cleansed of original sin and (in the case of one who has reached the age of reason) of particular sin; he is incorporated into Christ and made a member of His Body the church; he is infused with sanctifying grace and receives the theological virtues of faith, hope, and love and the gifts of the Holy Spirit; and this enables him to receive the other sacraments effectively. The minister of baptism is ordinarily a bishop, priest, or deacon, but in an emergency anyone can baptize validly. There is also the "baptism of blood" (which is martyrdom for the faith) and the "baptism of desire" (which is baptism credited to a person who had perfect contrition and implicit intention but for whatever reason could not have been baptized).

2. *Confirmation.* This sacrament is said to have been instituted by Christ when He promised to send His Holy Spirit and is fulfilled in Pentecost. When it is asked, "What must I do to be saved?" the answer given in Acts 2:37–38 suggests a twofold aspect: first, baptism for the forgiveness of sins; second, confirmation for the Spirit to be given. It is said, further, that Acts 8 and 19 provide scriptural witness to confirmation after baptism through a laying on of hands and reception of the Holy Spirit. Contemporary Catholic theology sees confirmation as the completion of baptism, a sealing with the Spirit, which enables witness to the Christian faith in a mature way.

3. *Holy Eucharist.* From the Greek *eucharistia,* meaning "thanksgiving," this is the sacrament of the body and blood of Christ, in which He is presented under the forms of bread and wine, offering Himself in the sacrifice of the Mass and giving Himself as spiritual food to the faithful. The *Catholic Encyclopedia,* demonstrating what we saw in chapter 5, adds, "Because of the importance and holiness invested in it by Christ Himself, the Eucharist is the chief act of worship in the Catholic Church, and the Consecrated Species of the Eucharist are to be adored by the faithful with the same worship due to God, because of Christ's substantial presence" (Stravinskas 1991, 369).

4. *Penance.* Popularly called "confession," this is also referred to as the sacrament of reconciliation (more accurately the "rite of reconciliation and the sacrament of penance"). The church, according to this doctrine, has been given the power, by Christ, to forgive sin. This sacrament is based on a three-dimensional concept of sin. Sin affects ourselves, our relationship with God, and our relationship with the church of Christ.

The Council of Trent defended penance against the opposition of the Protestant Reformers, who saw the priest as unnecessary for granting forgiveness. Trent, in response, required Catholics to confess all mortal sin by species (type of sin) and number (approximate) to a priest, who would then absolve them in the name of Christ and the Catholic Church. Vatican II reformed this practice slightly by stressing the healing aspects of penance. The new rite is celebrated either individually or communally (for several at once). This latter form is intended to display the community aspects of sin and reconciliation. Present Catholic Canon Law obliges all Catholics to confess mortal sins by species and number at least once a year and encourages the confessing of venial sins as well.

5. *Anointing of the Sick.* This sacrament was once referred to as "extreme unction" (from the Latin "to smear" or "to anoint") in earlier times. Formerly the sacrament was primarily for the dying, since it was administered only in extreme situations. It was often described as "The Last Rites." Several other sacraments actually include anointings—baptism, confirmation, and ordination. This sacrament is said to give strengthening grace and is no longer exclusively used for the dying in modern practice. The idea behind this anointing is to offer the healing grace of God to the infirm and the aged, to remit sin, and to make known the prayerful solicitude of the entire body of Christ for those beset by illness or ailment.

6. *Holy Orders.* This is the sacrament in which a bishop imposes hands upon a man, and uses the prescribed prayer, to confer spiritual power and grace to conduct ordained ministry in the Catholic Church. It is believed to put an "indelible mark" upon the soul of the recipient and thus can be received only once. Within this one sacrament are three orders: (1) diaconate, (2) priesthood, and (3) episcopate. Each is administered separately and with successively higher sacramental powers.

Deacons are ordained to a ministry of service and, in communion with priests and bishops, serve in the liturgy (service of worship). Priests are ordained with the power to celebrate the Mass, give absolution to penitents, administer the sacraments, preach and teach the Word of God, and fulfill pastoral duties given by their superiors. Bishops receive the sacrament as a fullness of their priesthood and are viewed as successors to the apostles; thus they alone have the sacramental power to ordain others. A bishop cares for the church under his particular charge as well as for the universal church.

7. *Marriage.* This sacrament was officially recognized as such at the Fourth Lateran Council in 1215. Theologically it is

considered a sacrament because it reflects Christ's union with His bride, the church. Unlike other sacraments, marriage predated Christ, but it is believed that He lifted it to sacramental status by His teaching and practice. Marriage is recognized as an institution of nature, good for all; but for Catholics who receive it properly in the fellowship of the church it is a sacrament because it is viewed as a means of encountering Christ in a special way and of bringing about the salvation of spouses.

For marriage to be a sacrament, Catholic couples must remove any impediments that might exist. It is here that the whole matter of the annulment of a previous marriage comes up, as well as related issues that often involve priests in matters that are difficult to pastorally administer. (This has caused increasing numbers of Catholics in America to pull back from the visible church after going through a divorce.) Both Vatican II and more recent papal documents have addressed the ever-changing need for better understanding of this doctrine.

AN EXAMINATION IN LIGHT OF BIBLICAL TEACHING

The Roman Catholic understanding of salvation, as we have seen, is plainly linked to a system of sacramentalism, which has been called "sacerdotalism" (of, or relating to, priests and/or the priesthood). To the average person who has not carefully studied the Scriptures of the New Testament or considered the effect of this system upon whole nations of untaught baptized church members, this system may carry a certain appeal. It has the appearance of awe, of mystery, of wonder—all elements of true Christian worship. But for those who are resolved to follow Scripture and the doctrine of the sufficiency of Christ alone and the gospel alone, there are serious problems with the entire system. These problems cannot be resolved by mere goodwill or ecumenical discussion.

As previously noted, evangelicals have historically held that there are but two sacraments *clearly instituted by our Lord* in the

New Testament. In the case of baptism we have an explicit commandment of Christ to practice this act until He comes again. Jesus commanded His church to "Go therefore and make disciples of all the nations, baptizing them in the name of the Father and the Son and the Holy Spirit" (Matthew 28:19). To obey Christ's command the church has always baptized those who follow Christ as Lord. There has been disagreement among evangelicals regarding both the meaning and mode of baptism, but they agree that Christ Himself commanded baptism.

In the case of Communion we also have the institution of the Supper by our Lord Himself. When the apostle Paul tells the church in Corinth to celebrate the Supper he quotes Jesus as saying, "This is My body, which is for you; do this in remembrance of Me" (1 Corinthians 11:24). The Savior exhorts His followers to do this in order to remember Him. Nothing could be clearer and more straightforward.

Where, then, do we get textual support for these other five sacraments? Did Christ command these in the same manner and with the same authority as the two sacraments just mentioned? I think not. I have read the scriptural texts often cited in Catholic sources for the other five sacraments, and I am left with a number of unanswered questions.

For example, where did Christ Himself institute these in a way that parallels baptism and the Lord's Supper? If He did not institute them, how were they instituted as sacraments? (The Catholic Church has sometimes argued that they were instituted by the apostles, but this legitimation is not *clearly* found in Scripture either.) History cannot show that these sacraments were directly instituted by Christ, yet the Council of Trent, in responding to Protestant doctrine, said it could. Honesty compels me to ask my Catholic friends to recognize that the ultimate claim for these five additional sacraments is the authority of the church. This authority, we will later see, is focused on the triad of the Bible, tradition, and the magisterium.

Further, the Catholic system of authority, with its attendant sacerdotalism, has made the Scriptures secondary, or subordinate, to these sacramental means of grace. Popular Catholic apologists often argue otherwise, but reality begs for a more honest answer. I would ask my American Catholic friend to travel with me to Brazil and there observe the reality of Catholic practice among the masses who flock to the shrines and holy places and wait for the grace of God to come down to them through the sacerdotal system of their birth church.

But evangelicals have consistently maintained since the Reformation that the sacraments (even the two that Scripture plainly says do exist) *add nothing* to salvation at all. Salvation is grasped by faith in the promises of God, which come to us supernaturally by the Holy Spirit using the Word of God alone. The written Word is a vast treasure in which the promises of God are contained and discovered by believing hearts. It has God for its Author and truth for its entire substance.

Despite the many dramatic changes made by Vatican II (1962–1965), the traditional Catholic doctrine of the sacraments remains fundamentally unchanged. (That is why I have used post–Vatican II sources in my notations above.) These seven sacraments are received as a means of direct access to God.

The apostle Peter expresses the evangelical view of the means of salvation plainly: "For you have been born again not of seed which is perishable but imperishable, that is, through the living and abiding word of God" (1 Peter 1:23). The verses that follow this text make it plain that the word he has in view is the word preached by the apostles and ultimately inscripturated in the New Testament writings.

In addition, the New Testament nowhere gives warrant to the idea that sacraments are *necessary* for salvation. I offer three reasons for this assertion:

1. God nowhere binds His grace to the use of certain external forms. Consider the following texts in this light: Luke 18:14; John 4:21, 23. Further, the New Testament has a strong anti-ritualistic element that can be clearly seen over and over again (see Matthew 15; Romans 14:17; 1 Corinthians

1:17; 8:8; Colossians 2:16–23; Hebrews 9:10; 13:9–16; 1 Peter 3:21).

2. Scripture makes faith alone the instrumental cause of salvation: John 5:24; 3:16, 36; Acts 16:31. Verses that appear to say otherwise are best read in the light of the clearer texts and the simple principle defined and defended in Romans and Galatians. The *objective* efficacy attributed to the sacraments, even if it is called "applicatory" in certain places, implies an addition to the finished work of the Lord Jesus Christ in His death, burial, and resurrection. The question is this: "Did Jesus fully accomplish the *objective* side of our salvation in His death, burial, and resurrection?" If the answer is yes, then no further sacrifice is needed, and any notion of the works of human merit, albeit made meritorious through infused grace, is completely foreign to the teachings of the New Testament.

3. The sacraments do not originate faith. They are not administered in order that faith will be *created* by them: Acts 2:41; 16:14, 15, 30, 33; 1 Corinthians 11:23–32.

Summing Up

Roman Catholic theology and faith displays an entirely different view of Christian salvation and faith than that of the New Testament. The church, in Catholic theology, is seen as an extension of Christ's incarnation and sacrifice. In this system, human agents are given power that belongs to God alone (that is, priests absolving sin, giving grace through sacraments, and so on). In evangelical faith, which follows the straightforward words of Scripture, true faith answers to the Word of God alone and takes the promises of Scripture as its own based on the "bare word" of God. Christ's expiatory (atoning) sacrifice is a once-for-all event. He is the perfect substitute. For the Christian who would follow the New Testament, the real need is to take Him in faith and trust Him alone to save.

CHAPTER SEVEN

WHO
REALLY SPEAKS
FOR GOD?

Serious evangelical dialogue with Roman Catholicism finds it virtually impossible to avoid the issues raised by the institution of the papacy. These issues were central in the sixteenth-century division, and they remain problematic for modern discussion as well. It is hard for many Catholics in the West to understand the serious concerns evangelicals have regarding the papacy, since they often think of John Paul II as a benevolent and kind gentleman who warmly radiates love for Christ and non-Catholics.

In a special commentary on the Feast Day (1971) honoring St. Peter and St. Paul, the Vatican radio declared, "The Church does not exist without the Pope. The Pope does not exist without the Church. He who believes in the Church believes in the Pope. He who believes in the Pope believes in the Church. Pope and Church are inseparable realities." This understanding, which sounds so completely foreign to the evangelical mind, is perfectly natural to Catholic teaching, with its fully developed doctrine of ecclesiastical authority.

THE PRIMACY OF THE POPE

The teaching of papal authority grew out of the church's early relationship to society around it. Linear historical succession to Peter (believed to be the first pope by Roman Catholics) is a matter that may well be debated till the end of the age. What is beyond serious debate is the clear influence early Roman law and cultural practice had on the church. This background helps us understand something of the development of papal authority over the centuries.

What can be seen, and this considerably prior to the Middle Ages, is an increasingly unified institutional church organized along lines both juridical (that is, pertaining to the law, in this case Roman law) and monarchical (that is, following the pattern of a single head, or monarch). An evolution was going on during these centuries that led, by the ninth century, to a church directed by the human authority of a single leader—a pope. The dogma of the papacy gradually developed until it reached its apex in Vatican Council I (1870). This dogma added to the rupture that took place between the churches of the East (Orthodox Church) and the West (Roman Catholic Church) on July 16, 1054.

This division, described by the *Catholic Encyclopedia,* happened "when Cardinal Humbert, the head of a papal delegation in Constantinople, placed a document of excommunication on the altar of Hagia Sophia, the cathedral church of Constantinople." Why was this done? "The official reasons for this were the removal of the filioque [a word meaning "from the Son," which was used to teach that the Holy Spirit proceeded equally from both the Father and the Son] from the Creed; the practice of married clergy and some liturgical errors (for example, the use of leavened bread instead of unleavened bread for the Eucharist)" (Stravinskas 1991, 707).

This division, existing down to our time, has been addressed by recent ecumenical dialogue, especially since 1966 when anathemas were lifted by Pope Paul VI and Athenagoras I. One of the perennial problems, however, that remains between East and West is the papacy of the Roman Catholic Church.

The same problem existed with regard to the division of the sixteenth century. Luther began his reforming efforts as a loyal subject of the Pope, but in time he concluded that the whole papal system was unsound. His language, often harsh and offensive to modern readers, must be understood against the backdrop of his times and the way the papacy responded to him. Neither Catholic nor Protestant should be proud of some of the language hurled about in the sixteenth century, and hopefully these vital doctrinal differences can be considered by us *without* the invectives of the past.

What exactly is the Roman Catholic doctrine of the pope? The *Catholic Encyclopedia* once again helps us:

> The Bishop of Rome . . . exercises universal jurisdiction over the whole Church as the Vicar of Christ and the Successor of St. Peter. The term "pope" derives from the Latin for "father." . . . In Western Christianity, this term refers to the Roman Pontiff, called His Holiness the Pope, who governs the universal Church as the successor to St. Peter . . . who possesses, "by virtue of his office, . . . supreme, full, immediate, and universal ordinary jurisdiction power in the Church (Canon 331)." (Stravinskas 1991, 761)

This supreme head of the Christian church is said to carry out his pontificate through the office of bishops, cardinals, and various other offices of the Roman Curia (a body of *official agencies* that assists the pope).

WHAT IS THE BIBLICAL BASIS FOR THE PAPACY?

Roman Catholic apologists never tire of quoting Matthew 16:18–19 when asked to defend the papacy. In this passage Jesus asked Simon Peter who people said He was. Peter answered that "Some say John the Baptist; and others, Elijah; but still others, Jeremiah, or one of the prophets" (v. 14). Then our Lord asked the disciples, "Who do you say that I am?" After Peter answered, seemingly for the whole group, "You are the Christ, the Son of the living God" (v. 16), Jesus told Peter that the Father had revealed this truth to him. Then Jesus added the oft-quoted words: "I also say to you that you are Peter, and upon this rock I will build My church; and the gates of Hades will not overpower it. I will give you the keys of the kingdom of heaven; and whatever you bind on earth shall have been bound in heaven, and whatever you loose on earth shall have been loosed in heaven" (vv. 18–19).

The Catholic argument goes essentially like this: Peter is the rock in this passage. Christ promises to build His church on the rock. Thus, Peter is the first head, or rock, of the church, and the popes (more than 260 historically) who have followed him (supposedly in unbroken succession) are the heirs of this promise to Peter.

Protestants often try to interpret the reference to the rock in a way that shows why Peter could not be the rock in this passage. Personally, I am in agreement with evangelical scholar D. A. Carson when he writes, "If it were not for Protestant reactions against extremes of Roman Catholic interpretation, it is doubtful whether many would have taken 'rock' to be anything or anyone other than Peter" (Carson 1986, 368). What, then, can we say about Roman Catholic reference to this text in establishing the doctrine of the papacy through Peter as the first pope?

Catholic conclusions from this text suffer from what Carson refers to "as insuperable exegetical and historical problems" (Carson 1986, 368). For example, after Peter's death his so-called successor would have had authority over a living apostle, John, a prospect that simply cannot be demonstrated. What is actually said in Scripture is that Peter was the first disciple to confess Jesus in this manner, and by this confession his prominence continued into the early years of the church (Acts 1–12). He, along with John, is sent by the other apostles to Samaria (8:14), he is held accountable for his actions by the church in Jerusalem (11:1–18), and he is rebuked by Paul face-to-face (Galatians 2:11–14). Peter is, concludes Carson, first among equals; "and on the foundation of such men (Eph. 2:20), Jesus built his church. This is precisely why Jesus, toward the close of his earthly ministry, spent so much time with them. The honor was not earned but stemmed from divine revelation (v. 17) and Jesus' building work (v. 18)" (Carson 1986, 368–69).

Though modern Catholics will point out that the pope does not speak infallibly on all occasions, and the pope must himself confess sin and be redeemed as a sinner, the truth is that the doctrine of papal authority, succession, and infallibility is still a major roadblock to meaningful agreement regarding the teaching of the New Testament.

The *Catechism of the Catholic Church,* in speaking of the epis-copal college of bishops and the pope, says,

> When Christ instituted the Twelve, "he constituted [them] in the form of a college or permanent assembly, at the head of which he placed Peter, chosen from among them." Just as "by the Lord's insti-tution, St. Peter and the rest of the apostles constitute a single apos-tolic college, so in like fashion the Roman Pontiff, Peter's successor, and the bishops, the successors of the apostles, are related with and united to one another."
>
> The Pope, Bishop of Rome and Peter's successor, "is the perpetu-al and visible source and foundation of the unity both of the bishops and of the whole company of the faithful." "For the Roman Pontiff, by reason of his office as Vicar of Christ, and as pastor of the entire Church has full, supreme, and universal power over the whole Church, a power which he can always exercise unhindered." (Rat-zinger, 233–34)

Here it is stated plainly: Authority was conferred by Christ upon His apostles, Peter being the prince, or supreme head of them all. From the apostles this same authority is given to the bishops of the church in an unbroken line of succession, with su-preme authority vested in the Roman Pontiff chosen as a succes-sor to Peter since the first century. But a number of nagging questions remain:

1. Was Peter ever in Rome? We don't know for sure, but even if he was it proves nothing. A problem, however, is this: when Paul wrote his epistle to the Roman church, why does he address personal greetings to twenty-seven different people but never mention Peter? Strange omission, I be-lieve, if he were the supreme head of this flock.

2. Because Peter's name was changed is no proof that he was now pope, as has been claimed. Jesus changed the names of other apostles as well (Mark 3:16–17; see John 1:42).

3. The Catholic Church always lists Peter's name first when it refers to the Twelve. The New Testament does not do so,

listing others before Peter on several occasions (Matthew 4:18; John 1:44; and so on).

4. Paul spoke of reputed "pillars of the church" in Galatians 2:9 and named, in order, James, Peter, and John. Peter was an important leader for sure, but plainly not the supreme head of them all.

5. Paul, the apostle to the Gentiles, worked independently of Peter and never refers to submitting to Peter (in some sense) as head over all. If anyone qualifies as the human leader, it has to be Paul, yet he never claims any such office for himself. Further, Paul actually rebuked Peter to his face because he stood condemned by his own actions and his behavior was hypocritical (Galatians 2:11–14). The unambiguous evidence is this—the headship of the church was not in a human leader on earth but in Christ who reigned above!

6. Nowhere in any New Testament text is there evidence of the office of Pope, and nowhere do we have the model of a person acting as pope, a very strange omission if we are to understand that the church is not a true church without this office and the bishops.

WHAT ABOUT INFALLIBILITY?

Most Roman Catholics are not aware of their own history in terms of theological development and doctrinal formulations. It comes as a surprise, therefore, when they discover that the doctrine of "Papal Infallibility" came as late as 1870 at Vatican Council I. Here Pius IX accomplished what he had earlier begun—the strengthening of his leadership over the church. At Vatican Council I it was stated that the Pope's decisions, when he spoke *ex cathedra* in matters of faith and morals, were "unchangeable in themselves and not because of the consent of the church" (Session 4.4; Denzinger, 3073–75).

Vatican Council II (1962–1965) sought to modify this doctrine by saying that the college of bishops *assists* the pope. Whereas the earlier Council had taken a more anti-Protestant stance, Vatican II seems to address dangers within the Catholic Church itself and to seek to reform modern practice. The fact is, collegiality (the idea that bishops collectively share authority) is still to be interpreted in the light of papal supremacy. *De Ecclesia,* a Vatican II reformist document, states this clearly:

> The college or body of bishops has no authority unless it is simultaneously conceived of in terms of its head, the Roman Pontiff, Peter's successor, and without any lessening of his power of primacy over all, pastors as well as the general faithful. For in virtue of his office, that is, as Vicar of Christ and pastor of the whole Church, the Roman Pontiff has full, supreme, and universal power over the Church. And he can always exercise this power freely. (p. 22)

This same document on the church, which comes from a section dealing with ecumenism and the church's relationship to Protestant churches, adds, "Thus religious submission of the will and mind must be shown in a special way to the authentic teaching authority of the Roman Pontiff, even when he is not speaking ex cathedra" (p. 25).

THE CATHOLIC DOCTRINE OF AUTHORITY

All Catholic teaching regarding authority in the church and in the life of the faithful individual centers in the previously mentioned triad—Bible, tradition, and the magisterium. This is often not understood by evangelicals who speak of "cooperation" with Roman Catholic ministries, priests, or churches.

The Catholic concept of tradition is vital to understanding how the Bible is used and understood. The word *tradition* (from the Latin word for "handing over") refers to the teachings and practices handed down, whether in written or oral form, separately but not independently of Scripture.

The *Catholic Encyclopedia* says, "Tradition is divided into two areas: (1) Scripture, the essential doctrines of the Church, the major writings and teachings of the Fathers, the liturgical life of the Church, and the living and lived faith of the whole Church down through the centuries; (2) customs, institutions, practices which express the Christian Faith" (Stravinskas 1991, 939). It goes on to say that

> the Council of Trent (1546), in distinct opposition to evangelical faith and practice, affirmed "both the Bible and Tradition as divine sources of Christian doctrine." Vatican II states, "It is clear . . . that, in the supremely wise arrangement of God, sacred Tradition, sacred Scripture and the Magisterium of the Church are so connected and associated that one of them cannot stand alone without the others. Working together, each in its own way under the action of the one Holy Spirit, they all contribute effectively to the salvation of souls." (Stravinskas 1991, 939)

According to the *Catholic Encyclopedia*, the magisterium is "the teaching office of the church." It was established, according to Catholic belief, in order "to safeguard the substance of faith in Jesus Christ" and to prevent the individual from "being left entirely on his own" (Stravinskas 1991, 615).

It is believed, very simply, that Christ established an apostolic college in His disciples who, unified with Peter as their head, became the teaching magisterium of the first church. The understanding of this magisterium and its limits, role, and work were ironed out in the centuries that followed, especially at the Council of Trent and Vatican I. The magisterium proclaims the teachings of Christ "infallibly, irreformably and without error" when it follows principles that assure its faithfulness (as defined, of course, by the church).

What this means, practically, is that Rome may alter matters that will change how Catholics perceive and experience the life of their church, but *fundamental doctrines* (such as those we have considered in this book) do not and cannot change. This is what has been meant by the oft-quoted phrase *semper idem* (Latin, "always the same").

In practice the typical Catholic never experiences the magisterium directly. He reads and hears of its deliberations and actions. Where he actually experiences the authority of the church is in the priesthood of his parish. Here the chain of command comes down to the level of how he or she must actually live and act to be a devout Catholic. Here the person receives the sacraments, receives forgiveness for sin, and seeks to know God through his church.

Even at the level of the local parish priest there is powerful connection to the structure of the Roman Catholic Church internationally. That is why we can speak of an American Catholic Church, but ultimately it too is intimately related to the *Roman* Catholic Church. American Catholics are prone to almost loose sight of this reality.

Further, all that is believed and taught at the local parish level is to be ultimately related to tradition, the magisterium, and the pope. That is precisely why the idea is utterly impossible that one priest, or one parish, can be *evangelical* and still be properly related to the Roman Catholic Church, as defined in its own creeds and practices!

SUMMING UP

There is more serious appeal to modern Christian minds in this doctrine than many evangelicals realize. We live in an age of independence and, often, the spirit of anarchy. Ours is the age of "personal rights." Christians who observe the spirit of our times might well find attractive a church with a supreme pastor who has authority over all matters and to whom we can submit ourselves.

Indeed, in every age the tension has existed between submission to one (or several) who has authority over me and my personal responsibility to exercise discernment and make personal decisions based on an authority that is above all present human and ecclesiastical structure. Many Protestants often have church leaders who have become virtual popes in this sense.

My reason for opposing the Catholic doctrine of authority in the papacy and the magisterium, and the more recently developed doctrine of infallibility, is not because I desire to foster rebellion, much less willful independence. It is because this very doctrine, like so many others we have observed, is simply not grounded in the New Testament. In fact, I would suggest that it runs counter to the teaching and spirit of the Scriptures.

Martin Luther opposed "Enthusiasts" (visionaries, prophets, and so on) in the sixteenth century in much the same way that he countered the papacy. Both, Luther maintained, sought to exercise an authority above and beyond the written Scriptures. Their independence from God's Word was the primary problem. The church does not give us "new birth," rather it is by the Word of God that we are begotten by the Holy Spirit (see 1 Peter 1:13; James 1:18). Further, we have but one true Supreme Head and Chief Shepherd of our souls—Jesus Christ the Lord! His infallible teaching is not found in the human creeds and decisions of a fallible church but in the Word of the living God. This is precisely why every great recovery and spiritual awakening in the history of the church has broken forth upon rediscovery of the power of God in the written Scriptures, not in ecclesiastical structures and meetings.

We can honestly discuss how we might accept churches with a papacy on equal footing with churches that do not, but ultimately the faithful evangelical must allow Scripture to rule the discussion. Catholicism's position will not allow for a middle ground either. Perhaps Catholicism will change this doctrine in the future, but there is no evidence at all that she will. For the evangelical who remains faithful to the New Testament there is no middle ground either. Truth and unity are not served by covering over this major difference. Truth is best served by recognizing the supreme headship of Jesus Christ (alone) over the entire universal church.

All human leaders—pastors, deacons, elders, whatever—must govern and lead only in a distinctly subservient role as "fellow priests" (see Revelation 1:6; 5:10; 20:6) with the whole people of God. They are to serve in a spirit of gentleness that honors Christ the true Head of the church. And they must serve with derived authority, living totally under the written Scripture and its final authority.

CHAPTER EIGHT

SPIRITUAL
LIFE AND
DEVOTION

Nowhere is the difference between evangelical life more distinct from Catholic life than in the area of Christian devotion and spirituality. For Catholics, spiritual life can be defined as "the life of grace anchored in the rhythm of the liturgical year's celebration of the mystery of Christ, His mother and His saints; nourished by the food of the Eucharist, sustained by the grace of the other sacraments and deepened by communal participation in the daily public prayer of the Church and the private devotion to which the individual soul is attracted" (Stravinskas 1991, 901).

As theologian Donald Bloesch observes, "Whereas evangelical Protestantism tends to uphold a theology of the Word of God, the Catholic and Orthodox traditions have generally gravitated toward a theology of the spiritual life" (Armstrong, 143). Evangelicals have given considerable attention to spiritual development and personal devotion to Christ, but in the best of its tradition it has always subordinated this devotional activity to the revelation of the written Scriptures. Only in recent years has a major shift taken place that prompts growing numbers of evangelicals to be occupied with a spirituality that is more Catholic than evangelical.

The difference between these two traditions, notes Bloesch, is in both emphasis and orientation. Evangelical spiritual exercise is based on the unmerited grace of God rather than on human response in the spiritual exercises of a particular approach. In Catholic theology salvation is usually pictured as a joint venture in which we come to God seeking His grace to help us in our endeavor to know Him.

In evangelical Protestantism grace does more than enable our free will; it liberates our will for faith and service. Grace does not simply bring us the possibility of a salvation yet to be realized; it brings us the reality of a salvation already accomplished. Our role is not to cooperate with God in procuring grace or justification but to celebrate and proclaim a salvation won by Christ alone (*solus Christus*). We are not agents of God's saving work, but witnesses to His saving work. His grace when it first comes to us is irresistible, for it breaks down the resistance of the old nature and in effect implants within us a new nature. The decision of faith is a sign that grace is working for us and in us; it is not the condition for receiving grace. (Armstrong, 155)

MYSTICISM

Christian mysticism, variously debated and defined, has generally referred to religious experience in which the believer arrives at a special union of love with God. This experience is generally believed to transcend a knowing achieved by the normal powers of mind and reason. It frequently centers on the desire to experience the "nearness of God" in a state that may be ecstatic. Its focus is the interior life of the spirit.

The stress of mystical experience is usually on having an encounter apart from either Scripture or normal church relationships. (In other words, it is highly individualistic.) Emphasis is on the transcendent. Prayer is not understood so much as asking and receiving but as contemplation, including acts of asceticism that ostensibly promote mystical experience.

Mysticism has often arisen in the history of the Christian Church when undue emphasis has been placed upon institutional church life. The mystical way offers opportunity for more direct and personal knowledge of God when He seems distant. Often, debates about creeds and confessions will push certain kinds of people toward mysticism.

All Christian truth is mystery. By this I mean that, even though truth can be formulated and explained so that rational minds can respond to it with an informed will, ultimately God's truth cannot be fully explored or even made palatable to natural minds. The simple reason for this is the Fall. We not only sin, we are fundamentally sinners in every part of our being, including our minds. We are not able to see and fully comprehend God, yet we can state in clear propositions what God has revealed in Scripture. These revealed truths can be expressed in human language so that truth is communicated to rational beings made in God's image.

Let me illustrate what I mean. The Christian church accepts the doctrine of the Trinity. We believe that God is one God, but that He exists in three persons—Father, Son, and Holy Spirit. We believe this because the Bible reveals it as true, not because our natural minds have discovered it. We cannot adequately explain what the doctrine of the Trinity means, or what it doesn't mean, at least in terms of the questions that remain for us in the face of revelation. We will never be able to explain the triune nature of God so as to satisfy every question. There remains, simply stated, mystery. Eternity might well reveal fuller elements of the mystery, but one wonders if we shall not still be left with a multitude of questions beyond human ability ever to comprehend.

Mysticism is the practice of a kind of faith that believes we can apprehend God *directly* through our subjective experiences, as by intuition. Mysticism believes that the curtain of mystery can be drawn back, to some extent at least, through a direct experience of the soul with God. The stress in this practice is often on the ways, or stages, of knowing God. Special types of prayer get me into His transcendence more directly; certain practices prepare me to encounter Him in the inner depths of my being. These are part of the mystical way of life.

Evangelical Christianity has sometimes fallen into mysticism, as in the Quaker movement and in much of the modern Charismatic movement. In contrast, historic Protestant evangelicalism stressed the use of the spiritual disciplines as the means for careful response to God's initiatives in Christ. The approach to God was viewed as *indirect*. This means that we come to God *only* through

Christ as our sole Mediator and by the written Scriptures, which are illuminated to our minds by the Holy Spirit.

An example of my point can be seen in the teaching of most older evangelical churches. Here the stress is on reading the Bible in a spirit of prayerfulness, with meditation included (meditation is not "repetition" or "centering" in this tradition). This older evangelicalism does not stress "surrendering my inner faculties" to the light of God through an experience of irrational love. Perhaps the best and certainly the most balanced evangelical teaching on this subject can be seen in the English Puritans. Here confessional Christianity is generally blended with the disciplines of practical godliness in a marvelous way.

Roman Catholicism has always welcomed mysticism far more openly than older evangelicalism. One needs only recount the claims of the saints through the ages—their visions and apparitions, the special visitations of angels, the place of Mary and even of the mystical Christ of visionary encounter. Closely associated with all this mystical practice are two important areas of Catholic devotion that we will consider in this chapter.

THE SACRAMENTALS

As we have already seen, the Catholic Church teaches that grace is conveyed to her people through the sacraments. Beyond this she has variously taught that there are both things and actions, which, when blessed by the church, become sacramentals, or "sacred signs." These are believed to bear a certain likeness to the sacraments. In them spiritual effects are signified and obtained by the intercession of the church (Stravinskas 1991, 848).

These sacramentals include objects such as holy water, scapulars (two pieces of cloth suspended on the shoulders), medals, and rosaries. Other sacramentals may include actions, such as blessings and exorcisms. Sacramentals can be changed by the church, which institutes them, whereas it is believed that the sacraments were instituted by Christ and are unchangeable.

In a most interesting and candid statement, the *Catholic Encyclopedia* acknowledges that "(Sacraments and sacramentals differ in) the manner of imparting grace (a sacrament imparts grace in virtue of the rite itself, while the grace of the sacramentals depends on the dispositions of the recipient and the intercession of the Church)" (Stravinskas 1991, 848).

Here we encounter what is once again quite strange to the practice of the New Testament. According to Catholic teaching, sacramentals have no power in themselves, yet they *convey grace* if the one who uses them has a right heart, or disposition. Here is a connection of external objects and actions with the mystical understanding of faith that is inherent in Catholicism itself.

I am afraid that in actual practice this subtle distinction is lost on many of my Catholic friends. Ordinary devout Catholics seem to attribute huge importance to the sacramentals in daily devotion. One reason for this is the relationship of mystical experience to the sacramentals. The sacramentals make a wonderful provision for mystical experience through something tangible, something ordinary. It allows the mystical experience to be readily available to the devout common person. Further, some of the statements about the value of sacramentals from the history of Catholicism add to the mystique of this. Here are a few illustrations of what I mean.

Pope Leo X wrote, "The Rosary has been established against the dangers which threaten the world." Pope Pius V said, "By the rosary the darkness of heresy has been dispelled, and the light of the Catholic faith shines out in all its brilliance." Popes Clement VII and Clement X declared that all who wore the scapular

> participated in a special manner in the fruit of all the good done throughout the whole Catholic Church. . . . The associates (wearers) of this scapular have received the promise . . . to be adopted by the Blessed Virgin as her favorite and privileged children, and to enjoy during life her special protection both of soul and body . . . as she promised to St. Simon Stock: "He who dies with this scapular shall not suffer eternal fire." (Lambing, 151, 173)

DEVOTION TO MARY

There can be no question that the place of Mary in Roman Catholic doctrine and practice is another unique difference between evangelical faith and Catholicism. Significant areas of Catholic devotion and practice are powerfully connected to Mary. The views one encounters range from a genuine appreciation of Mary as the humble handmaiden of the Lord and the mother of the man Christ Jesus all the way to strong, clear ascriptions of near-divinity to her.

Before we embark on a brief survey of Catholic teaching on Mary we need to understand something about the Catholic Church that has not been clearly stated previously. According to Catholic doctrine, the church is Jesus Christ "available." In its *Dogmatic Constitution on the Church,* Vatican II speaks of the mystery of the church first. As *Lumen Gentium* puts it, the holy catholic and apostolic church "subsists in the Catholic Church, which is governed by the successor of Peter and by the bishops in union with this successor." In this conception the church exists "alongside of the person of Christ" (Stravinskas 1991, 607).

Rome views itself as "one interlocked reality which is comprised of a divine and a human element" (*De Ecclesia*, 8). Because of this there is a synthesis of human and divine elements in Roman Catholic thought that baffles evangelicals. The great mystery of the church, according to this teaching, is that it is an actual extension of Christ's incarnation throughout the world. As noted in an extremely useful little volume, "Since Mary is a picture of the church, in exalting Mary, the Roman Catholic Church exalts itself" (Schrotenboer, 32).

The place of Mary in Roman Catholic devotion is similar to the relationship of the Catholic worshiper to the saints in general. Following the Second Lateran Council (787), Rome made a distinction between veneration due to the saints and the worship due only to God. Even as early as this ancient Lateran Council, though, Mary was believed to be in a class beyond the saints of the church. To her the believer rendered higher veneration, which places Mary beyond all other saints but professedly a little lower than God.

This devotion to Mary has occupied an important place in the mystical practice of Catholics for centuries. It is a well-established fact that Marian rituals and festivals grew as the early church expanded. It also would appear that the growth of this veneration was partly aimed at countering vestigial goddess worship in parts of Europe. The church in the fourth century began to emphasize a cult of Mary. Over the years that followed, doctrines gradually developed around devotion to the mother of our Lord. Some of these were officially accepted by the church.

At the Council of Trent (1545–1563), due to reaction against Protestant opposition to much of this growing emphasis, Mary's sinlessness and perpetual virginity were affirmed by the church as official dogma. Two other important doctrinal developments were later added. First, the Immaculate Conception, which refers to the teaching that Mary was conceived without original sin, was accepted. This dogma was recognized by the church only in 1854. As late as 1950 the Catholic Church officially accepted the dogma of Mary's Assumption, meaning that she was assumed, body and soul, into heaven.

The non-Catholic reader needs to understand that these dogmas are "doctrines of faith," which means *they must be believed* by devout and faithful Catholics. If you reject these newer doctrines as unscriptural, then you must also come to grips with this simple fact—you have rejected your church because you have rejected its authority to develop, define, and interpret dogma for the faithful.

Of all the Catholic teachings that surround the veneration of Mary, only the doctrine of the Virgin Birth is plainly taught in the New Testament itself. As noted previously (chapter 7), the answer to the question "Who speaks for God?" is at the very center of the canyon of difference that exists between evangelical faith and Catholicism. The Catholic Church appeals to the magisterium and the continuation of the incarnate ministry of Jesus in and through the church; thus it adds these teachings without clear biblical warrant.

In the early centuries Mary was defined as "the Mother of God" because of debates that surrounded the nature of Christ Himself. If He were indeed God in human flesh and Mary was His mother, then she was, logically, the Mother of God. So far so good—except that evangelicals would rather stay with the language of the biblical text and say that Mary was "the mother of Jesus, or the mother of our Lord." Why this particular insistence? Because, though she was the *human* mother of Jesus, she was not *the mother of God* in the sense of somehow giving birth to the divine being or having an equal or higher authority than He.

When the New Testament is read carefully, what we see is this:

1. Those who honor Mary best honor her son directly, not Mary (see Luke 1:48; 11:27–28). And those who truly honor her hear the word of Jesus and obey it (see John 2:5).

2. In absolutely no sense does Mary contribute anything to our salvation, according to the angelic announcement of Jesus' name in Matthew: Mary "will bear a Son; and you shall call His name Jesus, for He [Jesus] will save His people from their sins" (1:21).

3. Mary acknowledged that Jesus was her Savior and understood her own role in this simply: "Behold, the bondslave of the Lord; may it be done to me according to your word" (Luke 1:38). And in the passage commonly called "The Magnificat of Mary," she praises God by saying, "My spirit has rejoiced in God my Savior" (v. 47). Mary plainly sees Jesus as *her Redeemer*; thus she must have been a sinner like any other mortal human. Only sinners need a Redeemer. Further, her role is to be the Lord's bondslave, not to share *directly* in redemption in any way.

4. Jesus taught with equal plainness, "I am the way, and the truth, and the life; no one comes to the Father but through Me" (John 14:6). All human cooperation in salvation is a matter of giving men and women the truth of Christ and allowing Him, by the Holy Spirit, to bring them to Jesus alone! Jesus ushers those who believe into the presence of His Fa-

ther. His mother is never said to have any role in this redeeming process at all.

5. Not one reference to Mary as the "Queen of Heaven," or the "Queen of Mercy," is to be found in the New Testament.

In spite of all this, Pope John Paul II, in his encyclical *Redemptor Hominis,* included a last chapter titled "The Mother in Whom We Trust." In this document Mary is given an extremely prominent place in the history of salvation: "We who form today's generation of disciples of Christ all wish to unite ourselves with her in a special way. . . . We believe that nobody else can bring us as Mary can into the divine and human dimension of mystery" (Pope John Paul II, 56–57).

Evangelicals may well have overreacted by ignoring Mary's sterling character as revealed in the pages of Scripture. She is, no doubt, a model to us all of a humble servant of the Lord, highly favored by God because of her submissive spirit. In a time when men and women alike need a Christian role model, Mary is a wonderful example of simple trust in the Father's bestowal and grace.

THE SAINTS

Catholic spiritual practice also includes "the communion of the saints." Interestingly, the *Catholic Encyclopedia* says, "Paul uses this word [saints] for Christians in general (Col. 1:2). Strictly speaking, saints are people whose lives were notable for holiness and heroic virtue" (Stravinskas 1991, 860). Saints are made such through the church's officially declaring them saints by a process called beatification and canonization. These saints are in heaven but can be invoked, with proper devotion, by praying believers on earth.

Vatican II says that saints are those who are joined to God in "sharing forever a life that is divine and free from all decay." Saints, furthermore, "have found true life with God"; thus they "share in his life and glory."

Once again, a reading of the New Testament reveals that the word *saint* is not used in this way at all. Further, the mysticism that leads to praying through the saints or invoking their aid has no biblical warrant.

A number of serious problems exist when prayer incorporates the ministry of departed saints. The only biblical explanation sometimes offered is that we all ask other people to pray for us (intercession), thus invoking their help on our behalf. But surely there is wide difference between asking a friend to intercede for me in prayer, a practice revealed and taught in the New Testament, and invoking the meritorious aid of additional mediatorial helpers (the saints and Mary) who are said to appeal to the glorified Christ on our behalf.

The question the biblical Christian must ask is this: "Can Christ understand my struggles, fully identify with me in all of them, and adequately appeal to His father on my behalf?" The answer of Scripture is that He, and He alone, can so help me (see Hebrews 2:18; 4:15–16; 7:25). He is the High Priest of all who believe. Why would I need any other aid in heaven if the man at God's right hand is none other than Christ Jesus? Why would I need *lesser* help when all I need is in the greatest help of His own person and work?

Once again, the emphasis upon merit, experienced through mysticism, comes to the fore. Evangelical faith is satisfied with Christ alone, through grace alone, by faith alone.

SUMMING UP

The place that Mary and the saints have had in Catholic practice goes much beyond the teaching of the New Testament. Undue mystical interest in the saints seems to be on the rise in recent years. Since the declaration of Mary's assumption into heaven in 1950, Mary has been increasingly the object of much adoration and love in the Catholic Church. Older Catholic catechisms actually spoke of her role as that of a "mediatrix." Until such language is removed, evangelicals will never be pleased with this undue attention to Mary, which has immense influence on the practical life of multitudes of Catholics.

The supposed appearance of Mary at Medjugorje (to six village children) in 1981 has caused millions of pilgrims to visit this site in eastern Europe. Though the Vatican is slow to endorse such a visitation, the miracles associated with it tend to encourage it in other ways. Father Giuseppe Besutti, a professor at Rome's Pontifical Marianum School, commented, "The church itself is founded on an apparition—that of Christ resurrected" ("What's in a Vision?" 67).

The rise of miraculous claims associated with Mary and devotion to her is noticeable, and not just in the underdeveloped poorer countries. Even the Vatican acknowledges a rise in claims of "pseudo-mysticism, presumed apparitions, visions and messages" associated with Mary. One expert on Marian phenomena, a French theologian named René Laurentin, said in 1990 that there had been more than two hundred such events since 1930. Most are viewed skeptically in official circles, yet in the past 160 years the Catholic Church has authenticated fourteen apparitions as "worthy of pious belief."

What this means, in essence, is that Catholics are free to believe or disbelieve as they wish. Yet multitudes of worshipers still seek apparitions and visions, longing for some mystical encounter with God. A Madonna statue weeps, a Long Island grandmother hears Mary speak to her and relates the messages, icons cry, and Christ "appears" miraculously on garage doors, water towers, and, in one notable case, a tortilla shell ("What's in a Vision?" 67–69). In 1993 a suburban Virginia priest experienced bleeding from his wrists. Consequently, the stigmata of previous centuries are again a matter for the practical spiritual agenda of multitudes ("The Case of the Weeping Madonna," 46–51).

The church may be slow to respond to some of this, knowing the dangers associated with definitive response, but it still encourages this preoccupation in numerous ways. Even John Paul II, who has withheld comment, is quoted as "having made generally supportive statements privately" ("What's in a Vision?" 69).

The real problem, seen again and again in these observations, is that the doctrine of Scripture held by the Catholic Church allows this evolution of dogma to happen. That fosters the elevation of Mary and other related practices that fit comfortably into an excessively mystical spirituality. In the time of the Reformation the inventory of relics that existed in the church was immense. Calvin directly attacked this as the enemy of the gospel of grace.

I am personally convinced that fundamentally the problem will never go away unless Catholics conform both faith and practice to the clear teachings of the New Testament. This means that they will have to give up the mysticism that prompts it all in the first place.

As confessed so pointedly by the Hebrew prophet Isaiah, "To the Law and to the testimony! If they do not speak according to this word, it is because they have no dawn [or spiritual light]" (Isaiah 8:20). If we refuse the more certain word of prophecy given to us in the Scriptures (2 Peter 1:19–21), we shall repeatedly land in the depths of a mysticism that will swallow up true faith in Christ alone. We must seek guidance from God, but the mystical way confuses two matters—*how* we get God's guidance, and *where* we get it. May God's Spirit be pleased to lead you to search "the Scriptures . . . to see whether these things [be] so" (Acts 17:11).

CHAPTER NINE

DEATH AND THE LIFE TO COME

I n the face of the grim reality of death, the Christian faith has always offered a most profound hope to those who believe the gospel. The apostle Paul wrote to the church in Corinth, "Death is swallowed up in victory. O death, where is your victory? O death, where is your sting?" (1 Corinthians 15:54–55).

Christ continually encouraged His own disciples regarding the hope of life beyond the grave. An example is in John 14:1–4:

> Do not let your heart be troubled; believe in God, believe also in Me. In My Father's house are many dwelling places; if it were not so, I would have told you; for I go to prepare a place for you. If I go and prepare a place for you, I will come again and receive you to Myself, that where I am, there you may also be. And you know the way where I am going.

The Gospel of Christ is concerned with much more than this present life. Its hope reaches beyond the grave or its message is simply a hoax.

Both Catholics and evangelicals are concerned with life beyond the grave. The doctrine of both has much to say about this crucial subject, but what is said varies considerably.

EXTREME UNCTION, OR HOLY ANOINTING

As we saw in chapter 6, one of the sacraments that Rome practices is anointing, or what was called extreme unction before Vatican II. The Council of Trent anathematized those who deny that this sacrament is one truly instituted by Christ.

The Catholic argument is that Jesus had power over sickness, and the Gospels show how He gave that power to His apostles. Mark writes that the apostles "were casting out many demons and were anointing with oil many sick people and healing them" (Mark 6:13). The epistle of James indicates that anointing of the sick was continued in the early church community (see James 5:14–15). Few references to these actions can be found in the early church Fathers. One reference in Hippolytus says, ". . . that this oil . . . may give strength to all that taste of it and health to all that use it" (Bokenkotter, 241).

It was not until the fifth century that Pope Leo I (d. 461) indicated the developed tradition and a new understanding when he wrote to Bishop Decentius. In explaining the James 5 passage, the pope made several points:

1. The bishop alone has the right to consecrate the oil.
2. In the absence of the bishop, the priest may anoint the sick person, and this anointing is sacramental.
3. The oil may also be used by lay persons for a nonsacramental anointing. When we come to the Middle Ages the rise of references to healing the sick through this sacrament increase dramatically. (Bokenkotter, 242)

In the East the rite became more closely associated with the dying and the forgiveness of their sins. Because of this emphasis the practice was looked upon as final and was associated with *dying penance*. Bokenkotter observes that the West also followed this practice: "Those who received the sacrament and by chance recovered were bound by the ancient canons to severe practices such as abstaining from all marital relations, etc. Thus the anointing came to be called extreme unction" (Bokenkotter, 242–43). Vatican II sought to recover the earlier practice and to make the connection with the healing of the sick.

The modern priest is encouraged to confer this sacrament in a way that invites the sick person, and those present, to share fully in a service of readings and prayers while the priest counsels and assists the sick person and his or her relatives and friends. The purpose is "to comfort them and help them respond with faith and trust to the mystery of suffering and death" (Bokenkotter, 245).

Along with this sacrament we come to another death-related ritual that for centuries has been a Catholic practice. I refer to the wearing of the scapular. The scapular is two pieces of brown cloth suspended on the shoulders. It is an attenuated version of the Carmelite scapular that, according to tradition, was granted by the Virgin to Simon Stock, a thirteenth-century English monk, as a sign of his order. A Carmelite publication wrote that this scapular (to be worn by Catholic soldiers in military service) carried a picture of Mary, Joseph, and St. Simon Stock with the words "Whoever lies clothed in this scapular shall not suffer eternal fire" (cited in Carson 1964, 110).

WHY THIS APPROACH TO DEATH?

In spite of this ritual and extensive preparation for death, through both sacrament and sacramental, why is death still viewed by many Catholics as something other than a hopeful entry into heaven? The evangelical, contrary to this, reads the New Testament and finds comfort.

As noted previously, traditional Catholic theology and practice is given over to structuring, rationalizing, and preparing for grace. There is a strong strain of legalism in all of this. Christ's death, in Catholic thought, removes the guilt and corruption of original sin for those baptized. But this is only a "first" justification. It must be followed by a "second," which is based on love working out of the heart. The devout soul, especially if it is the soul of an earnest and well-taught person, is left with perplexing questions that gnaw at the heart.

"Have I done enough?"

"When I did that act of love and charity, was my motive right before God?"

And, most importantly, "How can I really know if God accepts my way of living?"

The person who ponders the question of life after death will not find questions like these in the New Testament. What he will find are words like these:

Therefore, being always of good courage, and knowing that while we are at home in the body we are absent from the Lord—for we walk by faith, not by sight—we are of good courage, I say, and prefer rather to be absent from the body and to be at home with the Lord. (2 Corinthians 5:6–8)

But I am hard-pressed from both directions, having the desire to depart and be with Christ, for that is very much better; yet to remain on in the flesh is more necessary for your sake. (Philippians 1:23–24)

But for the devout Catholic there is little hope of immediate entry into the Lord's presence in heaven upon death. Although purgatory may not be the desired goal, it is the hoped-for reality of most. Those who die in mortal sin, in a state in impenitence, go to hell. Those who die in a state of *perfect* holiness enter heaven. To this class belong martyrs, whose blood serves for final purification. In practice, the number who are believed to enter heaven *immediately* is a tiny minority.

The *Catechism of the Catholic Church* teaches,

The Christian who unites his own death to that of Jesus views it as a step towards him and an entrance into everlasting life. When the Church for the last time speaks Christ's words of pardon and absolution over the dying Christian, seals him for the last time with a strengthening anointing, and gives him Christ in viaticum as nourishment for the journey, she speaks with gentle assurance. (Ratzinger, 266)

The phrase "gives him Christ in viaticum" means to give him Christ in the Eucharist as preparation for his dying journey.

This sounds somewhat hopeful, doesn't it? On the surface I would answer yes, but in reality it leaves the devout with great doubt and fear. The *Catechism* even speaks a few words later of death bringing a person into "the blessedness of heaven . . . immediately" if they are in grace. But, it must be noted, the words preceding "immediately" are "through a purification." We are left by this teaching with a huge problem. Most of those who die in grace are simply not adequately purified to enter heaven without *further purification*. This will take place in purgatory, where "final purification" occurs.

What is the basis for this doctrine? The *Catechism* accurately says, "The Church formulated her doctrine of faith on purgatory especially at the Councils of Florence and Trent. The tradition of the Church, by reference to certain texts of Scripture, speaks of a cleansing fire" (Ratzinger, 268–69). The practice makes reference to several texts that should be carefully studied (see 1 Corinthians 3:15; 1 Peter 1:7; 3:19).

To say the least, the concept of purgatory is not explicitly stated in these verses. The passage in 1 Corinthians is addressed to those who "build" (ministers) the church, and the fact stated here is that they will face a stricter judgment regarding the quality of materials they used in building their ministry. The passage in 1 Peter makes a contrast between Noah's day and Christ's day in terms of judgment. The best suggestion, I believe, is that a parallel exists—Noah preached, people disobeyed, they were judged; Christ preached, people rejected, they are rejected. Further, the spirits in prison who were preached to were most likely those whom Christ preached to *through Noah* in his time. Regardless of how we solve the admitted difficulties of this passage, there is no clear reference to purgatory here.

Further reference is made by Catholic teaching to the apocryphal book of 2 Maccabees: "Therefore [Judas Maccabeus] made atonement for the dead, that they might be delivered from their sin." With this the *Catechism* also encourages prayers for the dead made explicitly at the Eucharistic sacrifice (that is, in the Mass). The *Catechism* sums up this doctrine in one short paragraph under the section "In Brief": "Those who die in God's grace and friendship imperfectly purified, although they are assured of their eternal salvation, undergo a purification after death, so as to achieve the holiness necessary to enter the joy of God" (Ratzinger, 275).

How does the evangelical who believes that Scripture alone is God's authority, and not the Councils of the Church, respond to such a doctrine? We reply that evangelicals stress the perfection, finality, and completion of Christ's once-for-all sacrifice at Calvary. We read such straightforward and hope-filled words in Hebrews 9:23–28:

> Therefore it was necessary for the copies of the things in the heavens to be cleansed with these, but the heavenly things themselves with better sacrifices than these. For Christ did not enter a holy place made with hands, a mere copy of the true one, but into heaven itself, now to appear in the presence of God for us; nor was it that He would offer Himself often, as the high priest enters the holy place year by year with blood not his own. Otherwise, He would have needed to suffer often since the foundation of the world; but now once at the consummation of the ages He has been manifested to put away sin by the sacrifice of Himself. And inasmuch as it is appointed for men to die once and after this comes judgment, so Christ also, having been offered once to bear the sins of many, shall appear a second time for salvation without reference to sin, to those who eagerly await Him.

Christ's death met the perfect demands of God's violated law. All who truly trust in Him alone to save them will enter into heaven, not because they have been purified over and over again, but because of the one-time sacrifice of Christ alone. To teach otherwise, we submit, is to suggest that Christ's death is not adequate enough to save those who entrust themselves to Him.

Further, if sin has been paid for, to pay for it again, in ourselves or in purgatory, is to pay twice for something. This means that the atonement of Christ was either not perfect, as the text denies, or that God is not just, thus judging the sin twice. The evangelical would say, further, that "the blood of Jesus His Son cleanses us from all sin" (1 John 1:7). How can further purging be needed when Paul says, "God displayed [Christ] publicly as a propitiation in His blood through faith" (Romans 3:25). Has Christ's propitiation for those who believe in the Son been voided somehow? No, for the Father has accepted this perfect sacrifice.

SUMMING UP

To get to the bottom line in all of this we must stress what was a central issue for the Protestant Reformers. It is still a major issue for evangelical Christians who follow the New Testament. I refer to the doctrine of assurance: "How can I know I am redeemed and that I will certainly go to heaven when I die?"

For the devout Catholic the doctrine of assurance is tenuous at best, if not totally nonexistent: You receive the sacraments of your church. You strive to avoid mortal sin. If you fail, you immediately confess it. You realize that venial sin is another matter, and you labor under its weight. You hope to increase your experience of the grace of God in the mystery that is your church. You are offered comfort in several ways. You pray the rosary, perhaps attend a Bible study, and give of your wealth to the church. But do you know, truly know, that when you die you are going to be His child forever and that He will accept you into His heaven immediately?

Listen to the teaching of Jesus Himself: "Truly, truly, I say to you, he who hears My word, and believes Him who sent Me, has eternal life, and does not come into judgment, but has passed out of death into life" (John 5:24). Can you not see the radical difference between the assurance this promise gives to those who trust Christ only?

I labor to avoid unnecessary offense in every way, but this doctrine regarding death and purgatory underscores the clear difference between evangelical faith in Christ alone and Catholic faith. Here is a doctrine, with no obvious biblical support, that causes multitudes to trust the visible church and its sacraments to save them. But in the end this very teaching gives no sure hope of eternal life with our Savior in heaven. I must offer my protest precisely because I love the Word of God and the people of God.

This is not a minor difference. It painfully separates evangelical believers from Catholic doctrine and practice. My argument is not with you, as a Catholic friend. It is with your church and its way of building traditions that are contrary to the Word of God.

PART THREE

THE CHALLENGE TODAY

Evangelicals at the end of the twentieth century are suffering a kind of historical and doctrinal amnesia. We do not seem to know where we came from or where we are going. We embrace many agendas without clarity regarding our main agenda—preaching and living the gospel.

Having increasingly put aside the old language and harsh rhetoric of the past, evangelicals and Catholics are now discussing unity and "common mission." Historic steps have been recently taken that excite some and confuse many. Further, some well-known evangelicals have converted to Catholicism. What are we to say to these noteworthy conversions?

If evangelicalism is to remain true to both its theological heritage and the Scriptures it still professes to follow, what can we learn from the great concerns of the Protestant Reformation that will help us keep our ship on course? Are these concerns still important?

CHAPTER TEN

THE
PRESENT
HOUR

T ime has a way of changing some things, while other things seem to remain the same. The Catholic Church has for centuries claimed changelessness for itself. Yet it is quite obvious that the modern church has entered the late twentieth century with a new focus because of Vatican II (1962–1965). For this most Catholics are pleased. It allows for a new kind of discussion, and it allows Catholics and evangelicals to talk to one another without many of the fears of the past. It invites us to listen, to learn, and to grow.

But with these gains there are also losses. One of the significant losses of the post–Vatican II climate is increasingly recognized by conservative Catholics. Rome may not be the same church (in style and form) that existed after the more reactionary deliberations of Trent and Vatican I (1870), but, as a result of embracing the thought of the Enlightenment, the modern Catholic Church increasingly looks more and more like liberal Protestantism. The creed is still officially upheld, but scores of scholars and priests don't seem to think the creed matters any longer.

Take for instance the radical work of the *Jesus Seminar,* shared in by both Protestant and Catholic scholars. The end result of this committee's labor is an attempt to destroy New Testament witness to the Christ of history, despite the fact that both Catholics and Protestants have confessed faith in the historic Christ for centuries.

The rise of modernist theologians in the Catholic Church does not bode well for the future of Catholic theology in the West. Protestant theologian Robert Strimple sums up the problem:

> The Roman Catholic Church makes a distinction between theology and magisterium, allowing intellectual freedom for theologians but reserving authoritative pronouncements to the magisterium. For the past fifty years the primary characteristic of Roman Catholic theology has been a desire to be truly modern in terms of post-Enlightenment theology. Recent theologians have called into question the meaning of every affirmation of the historic Christian church. Thus, the debate between evangelical Protestant theologians focuses on the most radically fundamental theological issues conceivable.
>
> Many points of comparison exist between modern Catholic theology and liberal Protestant theology. Of special concern is how Roman Catholic theologians have treated the crucial issues of scriptural revelation and inspiration, as well as the relationship between Scripture and tradition. Karl Rahner, the most influential Catholic theologian of our time, embodies this new Roman Catholic theology. (Armstrong, 84)

The average lay Catholic is confused by much of this, knowing simply that things have changed and that the changes are not always improvements. Those who study at Catholic colleges and universities will face the implications of this modernist challenge head on. The future of much of the Catholic Church is imperiled if theologians continue to follow the secular drift of the culture.

VATICAN II

Vatican Council II was convened on October 11, 1962, by Pope John XXIII (who died in June 1963). John was the pontiff who desired to "open the windows and let in some fresh air." He charged the council to work in three areas—renewal, modernization, and ecumenism. This general church council did exactly that, finishing its task on December 8, 1965. It was Pope Paul VI who presided over the last three general sessions and served his church during the early years of transition. Sixteen major documents, filling two large volumes, make up the written work of Vatican II.

Sometimes evangelicals argue that nothing was fundamentally changed by Vatican II. They argue that since Rome never changes

then surely nothing has changed, except a few unimportant surface alterations. Most who have studied Vatican II believe otherwise.

Though nothing central to the great doctrinal differences that
have existed since the sixteenth century has changed since Vatican II, what has changed is how the modern Catholic experiences
his own church. For most Catholics this is a welcome change,
though movements to restore the past are still active within the
church.

George Weigel, a Catholic scholar, writes accurately that Vatican II was a great revolution because of "the transformation of the
world's oldest institution from an instrument of the status quo into
an instrument of change." Weigel argues that there was a revolution in five areas (Weigel, 21):

1. Modernity	The church opened itself up to modern scholarship and thought.
2. Self-understanding	The church shifted its approach to lay ministry and calling considerably, thus opening the door to greater involvement in liturgy and life by nonordained men and women.
3. Liturgy	This includes, but is not limited to, the vernacular Mass.
4. Relationship to non-Catholics	This is the open door to all other Christians and even to non-Christian groups (ecumenism).
5. Religious liberty	The particularly American contribution to the church, this views the societies of the world as more desirably pluralistic in a sense that recognizes a more self-conscious separation of religion and state.

Our Sunday Visitor's *Catholic Encyclopedia* sums up the tensions of the post–Vatican II debate in a clear, simple sentence: "Debate over the Council's meaning has been a source of tension, especially where its discontinuity with the preceding Tradition has been exaggerated" (Stravinskas 1993, 955). This is accurate. It is also an understatement. The tensions will most likely not go away for some time, especially in the face of the radical new theologies that abound in liberal Catholicism.

At the same time Vatican II opened the door for new discussion with Protestants in general, and more recently with evangelicals in particular. Historic discussions have been held and important documents have been issued. For the first time in more than four centuries there has been meaningful dialogue without fear of reprisal.

But did Vatican II officially change the older doctrines that precipitated the great divide of the sixteenth century? Has Trent been formally reversed by these new developments? Not at all. A new formula has been adopted, a new way of thinking embraced. But the creeds of the past are left in place.

In liberal Protestantism all the creeds remained in place during the past century, but megashifts took place at the same time. Old words were still used, but they were given new and wider meaning. In this approach we still hear of salvation in Christ and of His death and resurrection. But what is meant? The old way meant that a real man died a substitutionary atoning death as a sacrifice for sinners. He died under God's curse and was buried. He rose physically on the third day for our justification. The new way speaks of Christ dying, but interprets His death as an example for us to follow. As for His physical resurrection, well, it makes no difference, since He(?) lives in our hearts through our experience of Him!

The new Catholicism reinterprets the old concepts, dogmas, and life in terms of this new way of thinking. The shift is from old, objective, distinct definitions (as found in Trent and Vatican I) to modern subjective experience. The circle is left the same but made much wider. The core is defended, at one level, but the appearance at the outer rim of the circle is significantly changed. For this reason the endless debate among evangelicals about the changes made by Vatican II is often wrongly informed. Because many evangelicals do not understand the Catholic doctrine of the incarnate mystery of the visible church, combined with the idea of the evolution of dogma over the centuries, they argue with one another about how much or how little Vatican II really changed things.

It would be far better if we listened to contemporary Catholic apologists and teachers, fully aware of our profound historic differences, but willing to understand one another better in the present environment. Vatican II did open a door for this kind of opportunity. The hunger for the knowledge of the Scriptures among countless Catholics is apparent. Should we refuse to teach both modern Catholics and poorly taught Protestants the great truths of the Word of God when this is our biblical and evangelical heritage?

OPPORTUNITIES FOR THE PRESENT HOUR

Dialogue is one thing. Meaningful agreement is another. Let's not kid ourselves. As we saw in chapters 5–9, major doctrinal differences still remain for Catholics and evangelicals. And the most important doctrines that really caused the great divide in the sixteenth century are still very much with us. (We will consider these more in chapter 12.) These differences are not minor. All of our goodwill cannot make them disappear. The house, simply put, cannot be united by an appeal to bring it together on the basis of our common denominators.

Opportunities for meaningful cooperation exist in both of our traditions. Catholics have seen an erosion of confidence in basic moral values among their rank and file in the West. Liberation theology and the rise of radical feminization, gay rights groups, and proabortion forces within the Catholic community itself all challenge the historically strong moral position of Roman Catholicism. As Catholics seek ways of pushing back these antibiblical challenges, they often find that evangelicals make positive cobelligerents in these cultural and moral battles.

Evangelicals, increasingly concerned about an eroding moral climate in the public square, find Roman Catholic moral theology well thought out. It is very consistent in its God-centeredness. Often Catholics reveal a deeper "fear of God" in terms of personal accountability than that encountered in many modern evangelical communities.

Ronald Nash has written accurately,

> Because evangelical social thought has tended to lag far behind the social and cultural writings of conservative Catholics, a number of conservative Catholic writers have occasionally functioned as mentors to a growing number of conservative evangelical social activists. A short list of such Catholic thinkers would have to include Russell Kirk, William F. Buckley, Jr., Frank Meyer, Michael Novak, Richard John Neuhaus, and George Weigel. (Armstrong, 187)

THE TIE THAT DOES NOT BIND

Because we have increasingly experienced unity in areas relating to public policy and cultural concern, and because we have begun to talk to one another in this new way, the tendency for some is to feel that we now have a common mission and purpose. Pope John Paul II, in his recent best-seller *Crossing the Threshold of Hope*, writes of this very thing:

> Many enthusiastic people, sustained by great optimism, were ready to believe the Second Vatican Council had already resolved the problem. But the Council only opened the road to unity, committing first of all the Catholic Church; but that road itself is a process, which must gradually overcome many obstacles—whether of a doctrinal or a cultural or a social nature—that have accumulated over the course of centuries. (Pope John Paul II 1994, 149)

The gains of the present discussion are real. So are the obstacles that remain. To speak of our differences as if they were not real is neither honest nor helpful.

COBELLIGERENTS OR ALLIES?

Over the last three decades evangelical leaders have found themselves working alongside various peoples on numerous projects and concerns. Sometimes this cooperation is political, as in framing concerns regarding foreign policy or international issues. Other times it is more distinctly moral, as in the abortion debate.

How are evangelicals to relate to Christians from other traditions, to non-Christians, to those who represent traditions plainly contrary to a Christ-centered theology of grace in the gospel alone? We may find ourselves working in our local communities with Roman Catholics, Mormons, conservative Jews, and Orthodox Christians. Should we avoid this involvement because we are evangelicals? I think not. Let me give an illustration of how we might think about this type of involvement and our relationship developed through it.

In the Second World War England was fighting against Nazi Germany and Hitler. America came into the effort as a strong ally of Great Britain. We had much in common, both politically and socially. Later, the Soviet Union under Joseph Stalin's leadership turned against Hitler because of the threat he posed against the Soviet nation. At the beginning of the war Hitler and Stalin had been virtual allies. Stalin and Hitler shared the common trait of treachery, and Hitler double-crossed Stalin during the advance of the war. This prompted Stalin to turn to England and the U.S. in his effort to repel Hitler. As nations, we sided with Stalin because of the mutual threat of Hitler. We were allies in one sense but never allies in another. Stalin was an ally, but it was an alliance clearly of a different sort than that between Great Britain and the United States, as Churchill and Roosevelt understood. To put it simply, we were, in actuality, cobelligerents with Stalin. We could never be his allies once the war was over.

This is the way the fallen world really is. Two groups may find that they can make common cause in important areas they both understand as beneficial to their mutual interests. But problems will arise when they expect the wrong things from this relationship, such as expecting their cobelligerency to become the relationship of close and abiding allies.

Let me illustrate further. Someone invites me to join a group called "Citizens for Life." I gladly join with a number of folks from various religious backgrounds. We are cobelligerents. Another group invites me to join in. It is called "Christians for Life." This is a different matter. Here we now use a word that has different connotations for different peoples. Evangelicals rightly wish to use the term *Christian* for those who are openly committed to the gospel of Christ and the authority of Scripture. But if they keep joining groups that use names and terms broadly, before long both the meaning of the names and terms will diminish. The name *Christian* already means little in our culture, and the name *evangelical* has virtually lost its meaning in the past several decades. If this continues, the reality behind the name will likely be drastically reduced as well.

Baptists and Presbyterians have differences regarding some important doctrinal issues. But they also agree on the doctrine of the authority of Scripture and salvation by grace alone. The fact that God is outraged by the murder of unborn infants moves them to be allies in the concern they have regarding abortion. In many cases they can be more than cobelligerents. Why? Because they share a common confessional stance and a common practical view of the grace of God and the Scriptures. They are true evangelical allies in spiritual battles for the Gospel of Christ.

Devout Catholics have a high view of life. This is grounded in their moral outrage against murder and their historical theological tradition. Because evangelicals and Catholics have such substantive theological differences, we cannot relate as true allies in the same Christian faith. We can be cobelligerents in important causes, and we can continue to talk to each other in the new spirit of openness. By we cannot, and dare not, overlook the differences that we still have between us. When the distinctives are surrendered, it is the evangelicals who will give up the most, as history demonstrates. We need to pray for greater clarity in this whole matter or we will soon lose far more than we gain.

But how important are these differences? Can't Catholics and evangelicals be more than cobelligerents and become real allies in the present secular society? No. Our differences are still so important that Rome believes that *it alone is truly the church of Christ*. Pope John Paul II writes,

> Christ is the true active subject of humanity's salvation. The Church is as well, inasmuch as it acts on behalf of Christ and in Christ. Christ . . . asserted the need for the Church, when men enter through baptism as if through a door. For this reason men cannot be saved who do not want to enter or remain in the Church, knowing that the Catholic Church was founded by God through Christ as a necessity. (Pope John Paul II 1994, 139)

When Roman Catholic documents speak of ecumenism and unity, we need to understand that their plea is essentially plain—we evangelicals may be "separated brethren" who can be saved outside the visible means of the true catholic church, but truth would best be served if we came back to the Mother Church. It is both the design of the writers of many these documents and the prayer of the present Catholic spiritual leadership that we (as evangelicals) return to the conciliar, creedal, Petrine Roman Church.

SUMMING UP

Historically evangelicals have believed that three visible marks determine a faithful New Testament church: a proper preaching of the gospel; a proper doctrine of the sacraments; and biblical discipline. Evangelicals cannot, by their own confession and faith, believe that Roman Catholicism is a standing, faithful New Testament church. Hopefully the reader can now see why this position is confessed.

We must not personally judge the ultimate standing before God of any individual soul. As Scripture says, "The Lord knows those who are His" (2 Timothy 2:19), and, "To his own Master [each person] stands or falls" (Romans 14:4). What we do insist, however, is that the New Testament is neither vague nor ambiguous when it reveals what a church looks like and what its message and practice is to be. We believe that Rome neither confesses nor teaches the apostolic gospel biblically. We believe that Rome does not administer and teach the sacraments properly. Because of these theological beliefs we are, sadly, obligated to conclude with the Protestant Reformers that "Rome is a fallen church!"

Because we believe Rome is fallen, we must urge Roman Catholics to trust Christ alone for salvation. We must continue to clearly preach justification by faith alone, through grace alone. This means that individual Catholics must trust in Him, not their church and its system of sacraments and personal mysticism. We believe that some Catholics may well be trusting Christ savingly, but, if they do, it will have to be in spite of the teaching of their church, not because of it.

How, then, should we handle our differences? With respect and in Christian love. We are obligated to love God fully and our neighbors as ourselves. Surely there is plenty here for us all to work at if we look at our differences without glossing over them.

CHAPTER ELEVEN

IS "EVANGELICAL" REALLY ENOUGH?

I n the name of common cause and concern there have recently been concerted efforts to express Roman Catholic and evangelical unity. One well-known example is the much heralded document "Evangelicals and Catholics Together: Christian Mission in the Third Millennium" (1994). This declaration has been hailed as a great step toward unity between Catholics and evangelicals. If the statement had simply been an expression of political and social cobelligerency, much of the furor it has caused would have died down quickly. The problem is this—theological language is plainly used throughout the document, and the gospel is not clearly affirmed in the areas where it should have been if unity in mission were the purpose. Sadly, many evangelical church members are confused, and a debate now rages, often with little understanding of what may be at stake.

"EVANGELICALS AND CATHOLICS TOGETHER"

The accord itself is a twenty-five page document prepared by some fifteen leading evangelical and Roman Catholic spokesmen and signed by another twenty-five or so leading evangelicals and Roman Catholics. It is neither official nor ecclesiastically sanctioned by any representative church body. It serves as an informal treatment of issues that are believed to be points for unity in our honest cobelligerence against an increasingly hostile culture. Full-length books, articles, editorials, and other verbal presentations have begun in earnest—all seeking to defend the document and the course outlined by it. Why the fuss if we do have much in common?

To begin with, the language of the document is theologically soft. It begins with a quotation from John Paul II that this is "a springtime of world missions." Then it adds, "As Christ is one, so the Christian mission is one." The implication seems clear—Catholics and evangelicals have "one mission."

But do we have substantial agreement between Rome and biblical evangelicalism on the mission of the church? Not if we take seriously the present theology confessed and practiced by the Catholic Church. Evangelicals may be "separated brethren" according to Vatican II, but the intention of the Catholic Church has been, and still remains, to bring evangelicals into communion with the pope and the ministry of the "true" church. For evangelicals *the mission of the church is to preach the gospel and carry out the great commission* (see Matthew 28:18–20). If we are faithful to our confessional understanding of the gospel, then we do this only when men and women are brought to Christ alone, by grace alone, through faith alone.

We confess, as evangelicals, that the universal church, the body of Christ, is made up of His elect. Such may be found in many places. Some believers may even be in places where the gospel is not preached. Some believe the gospel savingly in spite of the doctrinal errors of their particular church.

Because we love the church and believe John 17 (Christ's prayer for unity), we labor for the unity of the visible church. But we also understand that compromising the gospel is itself a serious sin. To talk about common cause and to refer to it as "common mission" with those whose church confessionally denies the gospel of grace is to seriously distort the message that identifies our mission.

Without the gospel there cannot be a standing church. (We remember that Luther correctly said that justification by faith alone is *the* article of a standing or falling church.) Rome does not confess the gospel. As we have seen repeatedly, she denies grace alone and faith alone by her constant mixture of grace and works.

Some individual Catholics may well agree on the essential elements of the gospel, but this does not unite us in "common mission." If we are to remain diligent for the gospel, I am afraid that documents like this will properly trouble evangelicals who are committed to the essential elements of their Reformation and evangelical heritage.

The document turns, in a second section, to areas of agreement. This is titled "We Affirm Together." Here there are areas of agreement in the arena of cobelligerency. The problem is that the document also states, "We affirm together that we are *justified by grace through faith* because of Christ." At first glance that sounds great, but do you notice what is missing here? The essential qualifier made famous by the Reformers—the word "only," or "alone." The evangelical cannot gloss over this omission without serious reservation and concern.

The document goes on to plea for greater visible unity and less polemical debate. Then areas of remaining disagreement between evangelicals and Catholics are mentioned. Here again there is a serious problem. Ten points of difference are listed. But, astonishing as it may be, the material principle of the Reformation is missing—justification by grace alone through faith alone. This is one of the doctrines that still properly divides us, yet the document ignores it. Also, other disagreements are not correctly stated. The result is an unhelpful misconstruction of our *real* remaining differences.

Finally, the document ends with two sections titled "We Contend Together" and "We Witness Together." Here evangelicals have further cause for concern when they read that Protestants and Catholics should not "proselytize" one another. This is regarded by the document as "sheep stealing." Some who signed the declaration have defended this statement by saying that it does not mean we should not evangelize members of other churches but simply that we should not overtly, consciously seek to lead people out of the church they are presently communing with. I am afraid that this is a distinction with a meaningless difference.

If Catholics believe they are in fellowship with the true church, in union with Christ through apostolic succession and Petrine leadership, then they must desire for me as an evangelical to come into union with the true church, or they do not really love me. If I, as an evangelical, believe that Rome is fallen and in need of both proper biblical authority (Scripture alone) and a proper gospel (grace alone and faith alone), then I must love Catholics enough to urge them to seek a gospel fellowship. I must urge them to make their conscience captive to the Word of God, not to me as a teacher or to the pope or to any other human authority.

I maintain, with my evangelical forefathers who carefully searched the Scriptures, that Christ does intend for Christians to have unity, but it must be a unity in the truth. Unity cannot be established with anyone who preaches a gospel other than the one delivered by our Lord and the apostles (see Galatians 1:6–9).

Surely both evangelicals and Catholics can be people of goodwill and understand at the same time that the gulf that still divides us is not *primarily* political or sociological. It is, and always has been, *theological*. The issues that we have considered in this book are not matters of style, dress, form, or ritual. They are matters of biblical and theological substance. To take a minimalist approach, which glosses over serious differences, will never lead to biblical reformation and promote spiritual revival in the church.

Some evangelicals who sign a document like this one are aware of the great doctrinal differences that remain between us. Why would they sign this document? My short answer, having discussed this with several signers and having read written explanations, is expressed in the following paragraphs.

Signers of "Evangelicals and Catholics Together" believe that they are developing an "ecumenism of the trenches." They argue that evangelicals and Catholics have many common doctrinal convictions—Creation, the Fall, substitutionary atonement, the infallibility of the Scriptures, and so on. Others cite the Apostle's Creed as a basis for common ground. They want to be sure that Christians are fighting the true enemies of the faith, not those who are fighting with them in the trenches in defense of the truth (Colson, 136).

Does this mean that the two great theological principles that have stood in stark contrast to Catholic dogma for nearly five centuries have been reconciled? Can we now form an alliance with those who hold to a confessional stance that opposes the gospel and the authority of the Scriptures? Until evangelicals again understand the gospel biblically, they will remain in grave danger when they engage in discussions regarding relationships with other communions and people not in gospel churches.

BUT DON'T WE HAVE TRUE CONSENSUS?

True and faithful Catholics believe, with their church's confessional position, that Catholicism is the one true church. They believe that it has an infallible authority in its magisterium, as taught by Jesus Christ. They believe that God has preserved this church inviolate in apostolic tradition from the first century till the present.

But as former Catholic William Webster carefully notes, "The claims for Roman Catholic authority cannot be supported by the facts of history or the truth of Scripture. In reality the Roman Catholic Church has departed from the teaching of the historic catholic church and can no longer be rightly described as catholic, but as Roman" (Armstrong, 284). The supposed consensus of the early Fathers is a myth often set forward and hardly ever seriously questioned. However, one scholar of early church writers, a Roman Catholic, writes,

> Sometimes, then, the fathers speak and write in a way that would eventually be seen as unorthodox. But this is not the only difficulty with respect to the criterion of orthodoxy. The other great one is that we look in vain in many of the Fathers for references to things that many Christians might believe in today. We do not find, for instance, some teachings on Mary or the papacy that were developed in medieval and modern times. (cited in Armstrong, 285)

Rome does affirm many truths that are catholic and apostolic. We began this book by quoting the Apostles' Creed, a commonly held statement that unites us in some important truths. The problem is with what Rome *added*—with what evolved in both Rome's understanding and practice. The evangelical believes that the problem is not with doctrines added by the Reformers but with the doctrines that needed to be recovered and those that needed to be rejected as well. We dare not add to the teachings of the New Testament. That is, for evangelicals, the bottom line (see Revelation 22:18–19).

Roman Catholic apologists justify their church's tradition on the basis of their theory of development. By this they mean that certain doctrines were *implicit* in the early church, but they became *explicit* as the magisterium defined and explained them over time. Evangelicals reject this claim outright. The principle of *unanimous consent,* by which it is argued that there is agreement among the Fathers in a particular area of teaching, will simply not hold up at many points where Catholic apologists seek to defend these added doctrines and practices. William Webster has ably demonstrated that "what we discover is not a *development* of truth but a *departure* from it. Roman Catholic teaching in its exaltation of tradition, the papacy, and the church is a depreciation of the authority of Scripture and the supreme authority of Jesus Christ" (Armstrong, 285).

The supposed consensus that evangelicals and Catholics have may well exist if we limit the ground of our agreement to basic moral issues. It certainly exists in truths such as the doctrine of Christ and the Trinity (see chapter 1). At the same time the great truths of the Reformation are no longer important to many who call themselves evangelicals. One reason appears to be this—many evangelicals no longer clearly understand what it means to be an evangelical. Another is our unwritten policy of working alongside virtually everyone in evangelistic efforts. In our zeal to get people into the kingdom we often fail to grasp the simple fact that the message of the gospel itself is the power of God unto salvation.

If we do not clearly confess, understand, and defend our message properly we will eventually lose our true power. We may continue to engage in political and social agendas, even adding that we affirm the gospel, while trading our very souls before the end of the decade for an agenda not worth defending.

IS "EVANGELICAL" *REALLY* ENOUGH?

A number of noted evangelicals have converted to Catholicism in recent days. When this happens a considerable interest is aroused among thinking Christians. Kim Riddlebarger, in an excellent analysis of this movement toward Rome, suggests two primary reasons.

First, there are those like Thomas Howard, formerly an English professor at Gordon College (Massachusetts). Howard, particularly well known through his own writings and because he is Elizabeth Elliot's brother, left evangelicalism because he felt "incomplete." A lack of stress upon history, liturgy, the sacraments, and aesthetics all attracted him away from evangelicalism.

Howard first became interested in liturgy in worship while a student at Wheaton College (Illinois). He refers to attending an Episcopal church and "feeling guilty about it." Catholic authors increasingly became his "tutors" over several decades, and finally he came to the conclusion that the Catholic church was "the appointed guardian of the Scriptures." Howard, in an interview with *Christianity Today*, argues that the unity between Christ and His church leads to the question of authority, and that leads to the magisterium. He adds, "Also important for me was the sacramental understanding of the nature of reality, the nature of God, the world, revelation, the gospel, and the Incarnation" (Woodbridge, 48).

Thomas Howard not only left a visible, local, evangelical church communion, but he also embraced traditional Catholic doctrine. He replied to a question by Professor John Woodbridge by saying, "I would espouse the traditional Catholic view set forth at the Council of Trent, which loudly asserts justification by faith" (Woodbridge, 57).

Like so many evangelicals who think they have so much in common with Rome regarding salvation, Howard does not show a clear grasp of the real issues debated by the Council of Trent. As we have already seen, Trent anathematized evangelical believers *not* for teaching justification by faith but for teaching justification by faith *alone*. This was the key word upon which the whole debate hinged. A host of other issues flow from this one little word, as we shall soon see (chapter 12).

It was Howard who wrote, while still a professed evangelical, the now widely known little book *Evangelical Is Not Enough*. I can still remember when I first read this book in 1984, shortly after it was first published. I marked in the frontispiece of my copy, "If this is what evangelicalism really is then I believe the author will convert to Catholicism if he is consistent!" Why did I say this?

Howard's book is a powerful apologetic against an American type of evangelicalism that has been popular since World War I. In this kind of evangelicalism, creeds, community, and history are virtually unknown. Certain doctrines have been made central to the faith, but whole areas of other biblical truth are left out. Worship in this kind of evangelicalism is man-centered (now entertainment-oriented?), while preaching is often nondoctrinal and anti-intellectual. I have seen a number of my friends leave this kind of Christianity, thinking that this is the only kind of evangelical faith and practice that exists. Sadly, I can understand why certain people like Howard convert to Rome, even though I am convinced they have abandoned the gospel in the process.

There is a second category of convert who leaves evangelicalism. This type can be seen in the former conservative Presbyterian minister Scott Hahn. Hahn's conversion (along with that of his wife Kimberly, the daughter of a famous Presbyterian minister) is well chronicled in their readable autobiography *Rome Sweet Home: Our Journey to Catholicism*. Hahn, who now teaches at a Catholic university and is a popular apologist for the Catholic church, converted because he embraced the very Catholic dogmas upon which the Reformation was initially debated.

His motivation was more plainly theological than Howard's. Hahn is a skilled debater and a well-educated and conscientious student. For Hahn the two great theological dominoes that fell were, in order, "faith alone" and then "Scripture alone." (We will consider these more carefully in the next chapter.) What makes Hahn so different from recent converts is this—he pushes his offensive against evangelicalism at precisely the critical points. He has understood that the Protestant Reformation was advanced precisely because of these two matters.

What can we say, in general, about these famous converts? First, we should seek to better understand why they left evangelicalism. Second, contemporary evangelicalism is in a state of general theological disarray, and this leaves it open to such conversions. The answer to this is to recover an evangelicalism that is virile, thoughtful, doctrinal, and God-centered. Finally, we need a better understanding of our Protestant heritage as evangelicals or we will continue to make the kinds of mistakes that encourage people to leave us.

We must remember that this crossing of the bridge to Rome has a reverse flow of traffic as well. Multitudes of people are going in the opposite direction—converting to evangelical faith and leaving Rome for a church centered upon the gospel. On this side of the street, names of prominent people can also be cited, but they are not as well known as Thomas Howard or Scott Hahn. One of the very reasons Scott Hahn labors as he does with *Catholic Answers* (a Catholic lay apologetics ministry based in San Diego, California) is that he and others with him are concerned to stop the flow of young converts to evangelicalism.

Those of us who labor in preaching the gospel have generally seen more conversions to faith in Christ among Catholics than any single group of people, both in North America and overseas. As long as the gospel is clearly understood, loved, and preached with compassion, I do not expect this flow to decrease.

How should evangelicals respond to these publicized conversions, as well as to the major efforts recently under way to unite our evangelical cause with Catholics in *common mission*?

A BETTER WAY

I would suggest that the better way to proceed is for evangelicals to maximize their grip on the gospel. We need a better understanding of the great, historic slogans of faith alone, grace alone, and Christ alone. We need to study the Scriptures with more openness and with the deep desire to be radically changed by them. And we need to seek understanding of the important debates that have shaped and formed our historic church. We dare not build our theology in a vacuum, as if we can study the Scriptures privately, without the input of those faithful men and women who have loved Christ and the gospel in centuries past. Here a proper consensus of truth must be sought and found.

The Holy Spirit will make plain to the people of God the truths of Christ's gospel if they search the Word in dependence upon the Spirit. This too is part and parcel of the evangelical way. This too has preceded previous great recoveries in the past. May another such recovery take place in our time.

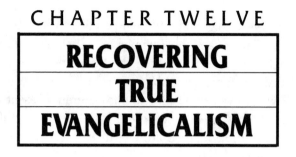

CHAPTER TWELVE

RECOVERING TRUE EVANGELICALISM

My assumption throughout has been that evangelical faith in Christ is in accord with the teaching of the Scriptures. It is, in a word, orthodox. In this final chapter I will seek to show why true, biblical, historic evangelical religion is faithful to the principles of Scripture and, as a result, why evangelicals must still stand outside the Church of Rome as confessional Protestants.

If we are to remain faithful to the Scriptures and to the Lord Jesus Christ, we must "contend earnestly for the faith which was once for all handed down to the saints" (Jude 3). If we will not stand where the church has courageously stood before and if we will not properly defend the faith, we will ultimately give away our greatest treasure—the authority of the Word of God. I do not suggest that we will do this intentionally. But if we do not speak with the clearest voice where the faith is under attack, we will run away from the battle and ultimately lose the heritage given to us by faithful teachers of the past.

If we lose our grip on Scripture, we will also lose our grip on the gospel. This message *is* our power. It defines us as those who affirm the evangel itself. This means that we believe people are made right with God through Christ alone, by grace alone, through faith alone. If we fail to understand and teach these Reformational truths, we stand to lose more than any of us imagines.

These great principles were at the center of the Reformation debate in the sixteenth century, and they must still be at the center of consistent evangelical faith and practice. They must be re-covered once again and not simply by scholars. An army of ordinary believers needs to search the Scriptures afresh and un-derstand that these are grand biblical truths. They are worth de-fending. They are worth teaching to our children. Present disunity and confusion only reveals our great loss. We have drifted far away from the truth, and we are charting uncertain and difficult waters as a result.

FOUR DISTINGUISHED *SOLAS*

As we saw in chapter 3, the Protestant Reformation of nearly five hundred years ago was fundamentally about theology. It was not simply a movement to purge the church of abusive practices, such as the sale of indulgences. Nor was it about claims to spiritu-al power associated with relics and visits to shrines. In this chap-ter we want to understand what the primary theological concerns of the Reformers were and why they insisted that these concerns clearly framed their theological positions.

Because Latin was still the language of the academy in the six-teenth century, the arguments of the Reformers were often framed in that ancient language. That is why you still hear unusual slogans such as *sola gratia* and *sola fide*. What exactly were the four *solas,* and what does each one mean?

1. *Sola gratia.* This expression refers to grace alone, or, liter-ally, solely by grace. Simply put, God's saving activity is outside of the human sinner. It is focused in the person of Jesus Christ, and the *sole* ground of His saving work is grace. Grace plus nothing saves the sinner. The grace that saves is given solely because of God's initiative, since noth-ing in people prompts God to save undeserving rebels.

2. *Solus Christus.* Christ's doing and dying on our behalf is the sole basis of our acceptance and continued fellowship with God. Even our fellowship with God must be Christ-cen-tered. The Holy Spirit's ministry is primarily to glorify

Christ and to make Him known. Christ is the *beginning* and *end* of Christian faith and Christian experience.

3. *Sola fide.* The Holy Spirit's gift of faith and repentance to the sinner comes through the hearing of a historical, objective gospel message and is received through faith alone. This means that Christ's substitutionary life and death is imputed to us for justification unto eternal life. The justified sinner receives the Holy Spirit through faith in the gospel, and the one justified will glory only in Christ's cross, making God's saving action in Christ to be the central affirmation of his Christian witness. He will be careful to obey God and please Him in all things revealed in Scripture through continual repentance. But his glory will never be in the feeble efforts of his own life or in the Spirit's presence within him. The Spirit within will lead him to look outward to Christ in every way.

4. *Sola Scriptura.* The Bible and the Bible alone is the Christian's infallible rule (canon) for all faith and practice. It alone is sufficient to establish the believer in the truth, and it alone will determine what he must believe as truth and what he must reject. It is efficient to accomplish the work of the Spirit in leading us into all righteousness. Its central message, namely, salvation in Christ, is plain for all to see when it is approached in faith. No creeds, councils, or human leaders can act properly in matters of faith and practice except they do so under the final authority of the written Scriptures.

These, in simple form, are the four great theological pillars of the Protestant Reformation. Much more can and should be said, but let the reader understand that it is for these great truths that we contend today when we insist on simple loyalty to the Word of God.

GRACE ALONE

Martin Luther did not rediscover the theology of grace. What he rediscovered were the Pauline texts regarding its true meaning.

And Protestant theologians since Luther have not manufactured a "straw man" for the purpose of ongoing debate. The proper understanding of grace is ultimately at the heart of every theological error regarding the nature of salvation. Either we have a religion that saves solely on the basis of God's grace, or we have a religion in which we share in that salvation. Our part may seem quite small. It may even be our decision or our human will that made the real difference. In the end, any system of doctrine that attributes anything to human beings regarding salvation challenges the sovereignty of God's free grace.

Medieval theologians wrote and spoke frequently of grace. What it meant for them was this—grace was something that God put within a human being so that he could cooperate with God, receiving the divine help that was needed to be justified before a holy God. Even Augustine, the greatest theologian of grace in the early church, was off at this crucial point, thinking of grace as something God put within the human soul.

As a good and conscientious Augustinian monk, Luther longed to be acceptable and pleasing to God. His problem was not simply an overworked conscience. He fervently believed that God was radically holy. He believed that God's law was perfect. He believed he had been given grace in his baptism and that he was continually given grace in the sacraments. He even believed that he must trust Christ as his Savior. The problem was simple— being a good medieval theologian, he believed that if he could apprehend enough of the inward grace of the Spirit in his own soul he would eventually be made righteous before God. But the more he looked inward, the more he saw darkness and sin. He was devastated. All he could hope for was God's judgment, which would justly cast him into perdition.

Modern readers often find Luther's vexed soul disturbing. We are simply not as aware of how far we have fallen from the law of God. We are led to think that God owes us something since we are not really that bad. If God will give us a bit of help we can cooperate, and all will then be well. Luther knew better. He knew the human heart.

On reading Paul's letter to the Romans he discovered that grace made a sinner right with God. This grace was *totally* different from an inward endowment. Paul declares that sinners are "justified as a gift by His grace" (3:24) and adds, "We maintain that a man is justified by faith apart from works of the Law" (v. 28). Later, he says, "To the one who does not work, but believes in Him who justifies the ungodly, his faith is credited as righteousness" (4:5).

Where Paul says in Romans 3:24 that we are "justified as a gift," some versions correctly say, "justified freely by His grace." The word for "gift" here means, simply, "without cause." God accepts the sinner quite apart from anything within him. Justifying grace is God's attitude of mercy and favor to lost, undeserving, rebellious sinners. Grace is not to be found in the heart of a person. It is in God's heart alone! Even when true believers reflect grace in their actions, they do so only as a result of this grace that is in God's heart. This is the perspective of grace alone.

If one insight distinguishes Luther as the father of the Reformation movement, it is this. Reformers who preceded Luther, such as Wycliff and Hus, saw many truths clearly but still lacked this perspective: *Grace means being totally accepted by God in spite of being totally unacceptable!*

But doesn't this mean that we can sin with boldness and without consequence? That is precisely how Luther's opponents reacted to his way of stating this great truth. And it is precisely how Paul's critics responded to him when he stated it this way to the Romans. After presenting the doctrine of grace for several chapters, Paul writes, "What shall we say then? Are we to continue to sin so that grace may increase?" (Romans 6:1). His answer is a simple Greek construction that literally says, "GOD FORBID!"

When we understand grace properly, it will raise this same question for us. If not, we have not yet understood or preached grace biblically.

CHRIST ALONE

The Reformers were concerned that grace could be used as an excuse for sin. The idea that grace springs from a kind of easygoing grandfatherly god who overlooks shortcomings and failures with sweet benevolence was unknown to the theologians of the Reformation. To Luther, for example, God was a sin-hating majestic Being who was terrible in holiness. He was able to cast both body and soul into hell. Grace, therefore, was not an act wherein God winked at sin and passed by it in simple kindness. Wrote Luther,

> Were this view true, the entire New Testament would really be vain and futile, and Christ would have labored foolishly and uselessly in suffering for sin. God Himself would have practiced jugglery and humbug without any need, because He might well have forgiven and not imputed sins without the suffering of Christ. . . . Although out of pure grace God does not impute our sins to us, He nonetheless did not want to do this until complete and ample satisfaction of His law and His righteousness had been made. . . . God ordained for us, in our stead, One who took upon Himself all the punishment which we had deserved and fulfilled the Law for us; thus He averted the judgment of God from us and appeased His wrath. Grace . . . was purchased with an uncalculable, an infinite treasure: the Son of God Himself. Therefore, it is . . . impossible to obtain grace except through Him alone. (Plass, 2:709)

As the apostle wrote, "Grace . . . [was] realized through Jesus Christ" (John 1:17). Paul sets this truth before us when he says that we are justified not only by His grace but "by His blood" (Romans 5:9).

One of the major points to be made about Christ's life and death as the sole basis for our salvation is that this view takes seriously the law and justice of God. No one could be justified unless the law was perfectly fulfilled. The death of Christ upheld the inviolability of the Law. It magnified God's justice fully. The law must be kept if we would be *justly* saved. Christ kept it fully and paid fully for all it demands of those who violate it. He redeems only through faith in Himself.

It is precisely here that the dangerous tendency to antinomianism ("against the law") is properly checked in the experience of true believers. We have come to Christ alone. In Him we are redeemed, and by Him we are kept by the Holy Spirit in grace.

Faith will not turn to sin as a way of life precisely because Christ has become our life.

FAITH ALONE

Even though justification and reconciliation are solely by grace alone and through Christ alone, not all sinners are justified and redeemed. Only those who take the warnings of the Savior seriously and look to Him will be saved.

Luther stated this well when he wrote, "Although the work of redemption itself has been accomplished, it still cannot help and benefit a man unless he believes it and experiences its saving power in his heart" (Plass, 2:706). If "a man is justified by faith" (Romans 3:28), two very important things must be noted about the faith that brings the believing sinner to grace.

First, faith is not magic. There is no saving virtue in faith itself. Faith does not make one right with God, it receives the gift that makes one right with God. It does not bring grace into existence, it becomes conscious (by the Holy Spirit) of something already there. It is, as one person put it, like opening your eyes to see the sun that was always there before you saw it. Opening your eyes does not make the sun shine. Believing does not magically make you a Christian.

Second, faith is not an attribute of the natural human heart. It is a gift God gives to us. He gives this gift to us through the preaching of the gospel and by the work of the Holy Spirit.

We must understand what faith is if we are to grasp this fundamental principle. Faith, biblically, is a noun that corresponds to the verb "to believe." Faith is the biblical term consistently used to explain the relationship into which the gospel calls people—a covenantal relationship of trust in God through Christ. Faith involves right belief about God. Thus, orthodoxy is a fundamental part of true faith (see Galatians 1:8–9; 2 Thessalonians 2:13; Titus 1:1; and 1 Peter 1:22).

Faith, furthermore, rests on divine testimony. Writes theologian James I. Packer, "The Bible views faith's convictions as certainties and equates them with knowledge (1 John 3:2; 5:18–20, etc.), not because they spring from supposedly self-authenticating mystical experience, but because they rest on the testimony of a God who 'cannot lie' (Titus 1:2) and is therefore utterly trustworthy" (Harrison, 209). But faith that truly rests upon Christ alone and the grace of God alone is a supernatural gift. Sin and Satan have blinded us. We cannot "see" unless God gives us light (John 3:3; 1 Corinthians 2:14; 2 Corinthians 4:4; Ephesians 4:18), and we cannot "come" to trust Christ till the Holy Spirit has worked within us, giving us both sight and the desire and will to come.

We must state this plainly: Faith does not save. A host of present-day evangelicals carelessly, or foolishly, misunderstand this point when they say, "You will be saved by faith!" It is vital that we state this as Paul does: It is "by grace you have been saved through faith; and that not of yourselves, it is the gift of God" (Ephesians 2:8). Please note the prepositions carefully: "by" grace and "through" faith.

Faith is resting, trusting, cleaving, and hoping. It is taking God's promises for what they actually say. In regard to justification it is taking God's declaration at face value: "To the one who does not work, but believes in Him who justifies the ungodly, his faith is credited as righteousness" (Romans 4:5). Present faith in Christ secures present "eternal life" in full fellowship with God the Father through Christ alone (John 5:24; 17:3).

This doctrine of justification through faith alone is an offense. It troubles the proud. It directly challenges the "good, clean, righteous" person who supports the church faithfully. It offends the person who considers his experience of God to be adequate for salvation. It bothers the victorious people who often speak of their ecstasies of the Spirit and visions of the supernatural. But to all who have struggled mightily with God's law and His holy character and have seen their own unrighteousness, this is the only hope they have—a merciful, good, gracious God, giving to them solely on the basis of faith. This is based on the righteousness of Christ alone by grace alone. Hallelujah, what a Savior!

SCRIPTURE ALONE

The assurance that God had spoken in the past and that He still spoke through the Scriptures gave the Protestant Reformers incredible boldness in standing up to the grave errors they saw in the medieval church. As Luther said near the end of his life, referring to the Reformation, "The Word did it all!"

The battle cry of the Reformation was "Scripture alone!" This truth formed the whole cause of the Reformation. It sustained the recovery, and it drove forward every entrance of divine light that brought revival. It will do the same in your life and that of your church fellowship if the same principal is truly recovered today.

What was it that made this principle so powerful, and what exactly is meant by "Scripture alone"? The Roman Catholic Church had believed, even on the eve of the Reformation, in an infallible Bible. It accepted the same texts as the Reformers, at least until after the Reformation (the apocryphal books being added after the Reformation had begun). What was new about the "Scripture alone" of the Reformers?

The new element the Reformers brought to the church of their age was the conviction that Scripture can and does interpret itself to the faithful from within—Scripture is its own interpreter. The Christian does not need popes or councils to explain what Scripture really means. Scripture has a self-authenticating authority within itself. Further, Scripture actually stands over papal and conciliar pronouncements, showing them to be untrue when they go against the written Word. Scripture was both *the only source and the only judge* of what the church had said and should say in any age. If we would speak with the Lord's authority, we must speak according to the Scriptures!

In the sixteenth century the authority of Scripture had been practically weakened in scores of ways. Human traditions were exalted, and the idea was that the truths of Scripture were communicated to the common people through the mediation of popes, councils, and priests. The Reformers in stating their great principle were setting forth the idea that God speaks to His people directly, finally, effectively, and authoritatively through His written Word.

Too many evangelicals turn to what their favorite teacher says or the best-selling book their friend gave them. They do not search the Scriptures as the Bereans of the New Testament era. We even add our own special set of cultural and religious rules and rituals, including a list that is tailored to each special area of the country. What we need is a great recovery of Scripture alone.

Did the sixteenth-century Reformers mean that the Bible was their only authority? Absolutely not. They appealed to history, science, logic, church Fathers, councils, creeds, confessions, and careful studies of Greek and Hebrew. But what they did mean was that there is only one ultimate, final authority—the Bible alone.

When the early church convened its first council to decide upon matters that threatened its own unity, the appeal was not to human authority. Its appeal was not to Rome, to one of the apostles, or to some higher human court. The appeal in Acts 15 was to "the words of the Prophets," which are said to "agree" regarding God's acceptance of the Gentiles into the visible church on the same ground of grace as Jews (vv. 12–18).

Thirty-three times the writers of the New Testament say, "as it is written." A most important illustration is to be found in regard to the doctrine of justification by faith alone in Romans 1:17, where we read, "For in [the gospel] the righteousness of God is revealed from faith to faith; *as it is written,* 'But the righteous man shall live by faith.'" Here Paul grounds his doctrine of justification by faith in the words of the prophet Habbakuk. Faith alone, in other words, is grounded in Scripture alone. Paul appeals to the authority of Scripture repeatedly in Romans (see 4:3; 10:11).

A particularly common phrase that indicates the same principle is found in Luke 24:44–47, where we read of Christ being written about "in the Law of Moses and the Prophets and the Psalms" (v. 44). When Jesus began to teach His disciples about all that He was and all that He had done for their redemption, He "opened their minds to understand the Scriptures" (v. 45). And in verse 46 He said to them, "Thus it is written . . ." If you read the New Testament looking for an appeal by Jesus or the apostles to tradition, creeds, councils, or church authority, you look in vain. In fact, such an appeal is condemned several times in the Scriptures (see Isaiah 29:13; Matthew 15:1–9; and Colossians 2:8).

In the sixteenth century, the authority of the Scriptures had been weakened by exalting human traditions to a place above the Word of God. The same problem exists in myriad ways in the modern church scene. The formative principle of the Reformation movement, and a major difference that clearly remains between Catholics and evangelicals today, is Scripture alone. This is true because the Scriptures themselves, and the Scriptures only, speak directly, authoritatively, and powerfully to the people of God. That is why, whether you are Catholic or Protestant, Christian or non-Christian, the Spirit of God speaks powerfully to your life when you read the Word of God in faith, study it in your home Bible study group, or hear it preached effectively.

A famous minister of the last century, when asked if he should defend the Bible, said, "Defend the Bible? Why, it is a lion! I would rather let it out. It can defend itself!" Scripture alone still says today, "Let the lion out! It is true authority, and it will be the instrument the Holy Spirit uses to bring people to the knowledge of true faith and holy practice."

SUMMING UP

Historian J. H. Merle d'Aubigne wrote many years ago, "The only true reformation is that which emanates from the Word of God." Ultimately the greatest fruit of the evangelical recovery of the sixteenth century may very well be lost to present-day evangelicals if they continue to turn away from the gospel and the Word of God.

Many important concerns face modern evangelicals. Our culture is collapsing. Values we hold dear in Western civilization are eroding. Secular intellectual barbarians are scaling our city's walls. Multitudes of concerned people wring their hands. Leaders continually call upon us to stem the tide. "Get involved," they urge us. "Do something if you really care." At times it seems that evangelicalism has been turned into a massive coalition of uniquely nontheological ministries all aimed at "doing something" to rescue us before it is too late.

My greatest fear is not that we will lose the culture, or even a great nation. My greatest fear is that we will lose the gospel. If we lose the gospel we will have a fallen church. We will have no real power. And we will have nothing with which to truly change the culture, one significant person at a time.

We no longer understand the doctrine of Scripture alone; thus frequent attacks upon this precious truth no longer alarm us. We evangelicals undermine faith alone when we ignore the centrality of this truth and its importance. We do this as well when we enter into agreements that turn away from this distinctive truth. We do this when we continually build ministries on something other than Christ alone and grace alone.

The answer is not far from any of us—evangelicals need to be evangelical again! Until we recover our lost confessional heritage, turn to the Word of God afresh, and plead for His mercy to fall upon us, we will continue groping for a center of reference. We are like a weakened and powerless Samson, going round and round in circles without our eyes.

A few rays of hope are emerging as increasing numbers of evangelicals become aware of what the Reformation was really about. Many see the significant doctrinal reasons for what took place. They dare to dream of another reformation impact upon our generation. They pray earnestly for a reformation that draws from the past, yet looks forward with hope. May God be pleased to light another blaze in the church that transforms culture with amazing effect.

A
PERSONAL
POSTSCRIPT

This book has been written with two kinds of readers in mind. First, the evangelical Protestant who still believes that the Scriptures really are the infallible Word of the living God. To this reader I conclude by asking you to "be diligent to present yourself approved to God" (2 Timothy 2:15) in every way possible. I urge you to grow in the grace and knowledge of the Lord Jesus Christ. You have a doctrinal and personal heritage in your faith and practice that you may know very little about. Learn more about it.

Seek to understand more what you believe and why you believe it. Keep a watchful eye on the events of our time that threaten to undermine the Reformational truths of your evangelical religion. If you do not know what you believe and why you believe it, you will not be equipped for every good work, and you will be easily led astray.

It is my belief that evangelicalism is in trouble in the present age. Not because we are not large, not because we are not active and vocal, but because we do not understand what it means to be truly evangelical. The tragic consequences of our weaknesses are becoming more apparent every day.

Second, this book has been written for Roman Catholic readers who wish to understand both evangelical faith and doctrine better, as well as the teaching of contemporary (that is, Vatican II) Roman Catholicism. My appeal to you is also personal.

Have you trusted Jesus Christ alone to save you from sin—
both its enslaving power and its fatal consequences? Do you really
know that if you died today Christ would accept you into His heav-
en? On what basis? If your answer in any way reveals that your
hope is grounded in your baptism, your fellowship with your
church, or the faith of others before you, you will not be saved.
You must trust Christ and Him only.

Further, do you understand that unless you are saved by grace
alone you cannot and will not be saved at all? God does not save
you because of your human will or personal decision. He does not
save you because you are a "good Catholic" (or a "good evangelical" either). He will save you solely on the basis of His grace, or
you will not be saved.

Do you see that you have sinned? Few Catholics I have met
deny this truth. Actually, Catholics sometimes understand this reality much better than many evangelicals. But have you personally
felt the weight of your sin? Has the law of God brought you to see
your helpless, hopeless, powerless condition before Him? If so,
cast yourself upon His mercy and ask Him to save you.

Finally, do you understand that if grace comes to you in any
way other than by faith alone that you are sharing in the work of
salvation? God will not share this work with you. Either He must
save you based on your acceptance of His free gift or you will not
be saved. If you contribute anything, even your faithful receiving
of grace through the partaking of sacraments, then you are not
trusting Him.

Ultimately you must obey the Word of God as the Holy Spirit
speaks to your conscience. For this to happen you must know the
teaching of the Scriptures. You must search the Scriptures earnestly that you may find the truth. You may well discover that
there are far more conflicts between the plain teaching of the
Word of God and your Catholic tradition than you ever imagined.
We have seen only a few of these in this little book.

If you follow the Word of God it may cost you dearly. Jesus
Himself taught:

Do not think that I came to bring peace on the earth; I did not come to bring peace, but a sword. For I came to set a man against his father, and a daughter against her mother, and a daughter-in-law against her mother-in-law; and a man's enemies will be the members of his household. He who loves father or mother more than Me is not worthy of Me; and he who loves son or daughter more than Me is not worthy of Me. And he who does not take his cross and follow after Me is not worthy of Me. He who has found his life will lose it, and he who has lost his life for My sake will find it. (Matthew 10:34–39)

But if you follow God, faithfully obeying His Word, you have everything to gain and ultimately nothing to lose, for Jesus also said, "Everyone who confesses Me before men, I will also confess him before My Father who is in heaven" (v. 32).

WORKS CITED

Armstrong, John. *Roman Catholicism: Evangelical Protestants Analyze What Divides and Unites Us.* Chicago: Moody, 1994.

Bokenkotter, Thomas. *Essential Catholicism: Dynamics of Faith and Belief.* New York: Doubleday, 1986.

Carson, D. A. "Matthew." In *Expositor's Bible Commentary.* Vol. 8. Edited by Frank E. Gaebelein. Grand Rapids: Zondervan, 1986.

Carson, H. M. *Roman Catholicism Today.* Grand Rapids: Eerdmans, 1964.

"The Case of the Weeping Madonna." *U.S. News & World Report,* 29 March 1993.

A Catechism of Christian Doctrine. Rev. ed. London: Catholic Truth Society, 1985.

Colson, Charles. "Charles Colson" (column). *Christianity Today,* 14 November 1994.

"Evangelicals and Catholics Together: The Christian Mission in the Third Millennium." Institute on Religion and Public Life, 1994.

Hahn, Scott. *Rome Sweet Home: Our Journey to Catholicism.* San Francisco: Ignatius, 1993.

Harrison, Everett F., ed. *Baker's Dictionary of Theology.* Grand Rapids: Baker, 1985.

Howard, Thomas. *Evangelical Is Not Enough.* San Francisco: Ignatius, 1984.

Keating, Karl. *What Catholics Really Believe: Setting the Record Straight.* Ann Arbor, Mich.: Servant, 1992.

Johnson, Paul. *The History of Christianity.* London: Weidenfeld & Nicholson, 1976.

Lambing, A. A. *Sacramentals of the Catholic Church.* New York: Benzinger Bros., 1892.

Plass, Ewald M., ed. *What Luther Says: A Practical-in-Home Anthology for the Active Christian.* St. Louis: Concordia, 1987.

Pope John Paul II. *Crossing the Threshold of Hope.* New York: Knopf, 1994.

Pope John Paul II. *Redemptor Hominis.* Boston, Mass.: The Daughters of St. Paul, n.d.

Ratzinger, Joseph Cardinal, ed. *Catechism of the Catholic Church.* New York: Catholic Book Publishing Co., 1994.

Stravinskas, Peter M., ed. *Catholic Dictionary.* Huntingdon, Ind.: Our Sunday Visitor, 1993.

_____. *Catholic Encyclopedia.* Huntingdon, Ind.: Our Sunday Visitor, 1991.

"What's in a Vision?" *U.S. News & World Report,* 12 March 1990.

Schaff, Philip, and J. J. Herzog. *The New Schaff-Herzog Encyclopedia of Religious Knowledge.* Reprint. Grand Rapids: Baker, 1977.

Schrotenboer, Paul G. *Roman Catholicism: A Contemporary Evangelical Perspective.* Grand Rapids: Baker, 1989.

Weigel, George. "Post Vatican II." *Eternity* (October 1986).

Woodbridge, John D. "Why Did Thomas Howard Become a Roman Catholic?" *Christianity Today,* 17 May 1985.

FOR FURTHER READING

For those who might wish to study the subject of Catholicism and evangelical Christianity, there are several books that may provide useful resource material. For those who are beginners I would suggest the following evangelical treatments:

Schrotenboer, Paul G., ed. *Roman Catholicism: A Contemporary Evangelical Perspective.* Grand Rapids: Baker, 1989.

This small book (99 pages), which is the result of a study done by members of the World Evangelical Fellowship Theology Commission, carries a lot of very informed and useful interaction with contemporary Catholicism.

Webster, William. *Salvation: The Bible and Roman Catholicism.* Carlisle, Penn.: Banner of Truth, 1990.

The author, a former Catholic, has done extensive research, understands his subject well, and writes lucidly. Highly recommended.

Coffey, Tony. *Once a Catholic.* Eugene, Oreg.: Harvest House, 1993.

This is written by an Irish evangelical minister who left Roman Catholicism and maintains a genuine love for his former fellowship and its people.

Regarding Roman Catholic resources for beginners, I would recommend the following:

Ratzinger, Joseph Cardinal, ed. *Catechism of the Catholic Church.* New York: Catholic Book Publishing Co., 1994.

Not so much an old question-and-answer catechism in simple form but rather a systematic treatment of post–Vatican II theology, both belief and practice. The definitive source for the study of the current teaching of the magisterium and Pope John Paul II.

Bokenkotter, Thomas. *Essential Catholicism: Dynamics of Faith and Belief.* New York: Doubleday, 1986.

A very readable and easy-to-handle book, which explains and defends Catholic belief succinctly.

Keating, Karl. *What Catholics Really Believe: Setting the Record Straight.* Ann Arbor, Mich.: Servant, 1992.

Accomplishes well the author's stated purpose—clarifying mistaken notions about Catholic belief and practice commonly held by both Catholics and Protestants.

For more academic study of Roman Catholicism written by evangelical authors, I would recommend the following:

Armstrong, John H., ed. *Roman Catholicism: Evangelical Protestants Analyze What Divides and Unites Us.* Chicago: Moody, 1994.

A conciliatory treatment that takes seriously post–Vatican II changes but strives to explain and defend Reformation theology.

Althaus, Paul. *The Theology of Martin Luther.* Philadelphia: Fortress, 1966.

An important work that will help the serious student understand how Luther's theological insights shaped the Protestant response to Roman Catholic doctrines.

For more academic study of Roman Catholicism written by Catholic scholars I would recommend the following:

Hastings, Adrian, ed. *Modern Catholicism: Vatican II and After.* New York: Oxford Univ. Press, 1991.

An authoritative one-volume guide to the Catholic Church and its development over the past twenty-five years. A must for serious readers who want to understand Catholic thought and life today.

Ratzinger, Joseph Cardinal. *Principles of Catholic Theology: Building Stones for a Fundamental Theology.* San Francisco: Ignatius, 1982.

The leading contemporary defender of the magisterium's doctrine provides a must book for modern reflection.

The reader should understand that this is a short list of resources and that the author endorses none of them in their entirety but merely recommends them as learning resources.